Uplifting Christ Through Autumn

Sermons for the Fall Season

Michael D. Wuchter

CSS Publishing Company, Inc., Lima, Ohio

Copyright © 2006 by
CSS Publishing Company, Inc.
Lima, Ohio

Some scripture quotations are from the *New Revised Standard Version of the Bible*, copyright 1989 by the Division of Christian Education of the National Council of the Churches of Christ in the USA. Used by permission.

Some scripture quotations are from the Revised English Bible copyright © Oxford University Press and Cambridge University Press, 1989. Used by permission.

Some scripture quotations are from the Good News Bible, in Today's English Version. Copyright © American Bible Society, 1966, 1971, 1976. Used by permission.

Library of Congress Cataloging-in-Publication Data

Wuchter, Michael D.
   Uplifting Christ through autumn : sermons for the fall season / Michael D. Wuchter.
     p. cm.
   ISBN 0-7880-2410-8 (perfect bound : alk. paper)
   1. Lutheran Church—Sermons. 2. Church year sermons. 3. Sermons, American—20th century. I. Title.

   BX8066.W83U65 2006
   252'.041—dc22

2006018179

For more information about CSS Publishing Company resources, visit our website at www.csspub.com or email us at custserv@csspub.com or call (800) 241-4056.

Cover design by Barbara Spencer
ISBN-13: 978-0-7880-2410-8
ISBN-10: 0-7880-2410-8

PRINTED IN U.S.A.

With love and thanksgiving for Michael's parents
Reverend Robert Zimmerman Wuchter and
Eleanor Joyce Freed Wuchter

for his paternal grandparents
Reverend Moses LeRoy Wuchter and
May Zinn Zimmerman Wuchter

and for his maternal grandparents
Henry Groff Freed and
Bertha Dubbs George Freed

Table Of Contents

Introduction

Soon after my husband died, I remember thinking, "If only his sermons were published, his passion for the Word and his unrelenting desire to relate the messages from the Bible to everyday life would be extended, and his ministry could go on."

Perhaps, because he died so suddenly of a heart attack in a remote area of Nambia, Africa, just as we were about to meet a delegate from our companion congregation there, I was traumatized. The people, however, learning of the situation, formed a prayer circle and sang hymns in their tribal language, some with familiar tunes. Christians extending their love and comfort immediately embraced me.

Once home, I mourned my husband of thirty years and when I went to church at First Lutheran in Duluth, Minnesota, I longed to see my husband up front leading the service as senior pastor. I instinctively looked up some sermons, but reading them brought more sorrow than comfort, at first. Over time, however, they brought nurture and strength. Each year since, I read more of them and was fed by them.

In time, as I recalled his ministry, I saw God's work at hand. As a third generation pastor, he embraced parish ministry at Resurrection Lutheran Church in Hamilton Square, New Jersey, with a sureness and devotion. After seven years, his call to our alma mater, Wittenberg University in Springfield, Ohio, seemed like a natural progression. Eighteen years later, parish ministry tugged at his heart to complete the circle. In every setting, his style was to shepherd the flock.

In the course of collecting sermons appropriate for the end of the church year, I decided to form a ritual. I disciplined myself to write a reaction to each sermon. In journal form, I responded to theological thoughts, reminisced about the circumstances surrounding his vignettes, touched upon some precious family memories, and even discovered a few new things about my beloved.

At one point I wrote, "I love reading his sermons and being enmeshed in his words and ideas." I felt wrapped in his presence. I felt connected. I was establishing a new relationship with him. I found that his words helped clarify my own beliefs, stretched my thinking, and energized me. I wish the same for others.

Shirley Dyer Wuchter

To Betty —

Rejoice in the WORD!

Shirley Dyer Wuchter

Holy Cross Day
1 Corinthians 1:18-24; John 12:20-23

Scandal Of The Cross

In the gospel reading in John, the author portrays the anticipation and struggle within the person of Jesus before his death by crucifixion. In the midst of the resurrection words of glorification and victory come some trapped words of crucifixion.

> *Now my soul is in turmoil, and what am I to say? Father save me from this hour ... now shall the Prince of this world be driven out ... this he said to indicate the kind of death he was to die.*
> — John 12:27-33 (paraphrased)

If the reading would have been allowed to continue, in the next verse the listening crowd responded to Jesus — "Our law tells us that the Messiah will live forever."

Today in the church year is Holy Cross Day — what is this holy cross?

If you discreetly, or not so discreetly, check out the necks of those who pass by you on the way to the theater, or the necks of those who pass by your vision on the movie screen, or through the pages of a magazine, you will, quite often, notice a cross on a chain. What is this that chokes the neck and accents the breast of so many people today?

For some it is a statement of strong faith; for others, a matter of style; for some a bit of family nostalgia; or a gift from a friend; for some a symbolic search; and for others that miniature cross holds a greater power.

The cross, silver or gold, carved wood, mosaic, a chip of a diamond, or soldered metal — what is this cross?

9

In June of 1968 in the aftermath of the Six-Day War, a rocky hillside north of Old Jerusalem's Damascus Gate was in the process of being bulldozed flat in preparation for the erection of a modern apartment house complex. Apartment buildings seem to grow well in dry, rocky Palestinian soil. But almost immediately, as the earth eaters bit into the hillside, it was discovered that the site was honeycombed with burial caves dating back to the New Testament period. They found fifteen ossuaries or small, stone coffins which held the skeletons of 35 people — eleven men, twelve women, and twelve children.

At least five of the buried Judeans had met violent deaths. In one ossuary, in addition to the dust of time, were the bones of a child, and those of an adult male whose name was Yebohanan — John. It was inscribed in Aramaic on the outside of the container.

In the spirit of Sherlock Homes, with the power of today's scientific intrusion into things, it seems that no secrets can be kept, not even the secrets of the grave.

John's bone structure paints a rather detailed picture of the young man. According to the story locked in the bones, John was in his mid-twenties at the time of his death. He would have stood about five-foot, five-inches tall, about average male height for the period.

His only deformities were a very slight cleft palate and a barely perceptible asymmetry of the skull — the possible sign of a difficult birth. John would have probably been a Caesarean section baby today, but he matured into a strong young man and seemed to have been in exceptionally good health. He had fine, delicate, good-looking features — he would have probably worn a well-trimmed beard. The bond joints imply he had never performed hard labor. He had upper class, educated origins; he was a college student type.

One thing more, though, from the record — something that sets John apart from all the other imprints of past life that now fertilize our hills and valleys — John's heel bones were penetrated by the rusting remains of a seven inch long nail.

This John, it appears, had met death slowly and painfully on a cross. What had been uncovered along with John was the first firm physical evidence of an actual Roman crucifixion in the ancient Mediterranean world although recorded secular and period history objectively documents crucifixion as a rather common form of capital punishment.

The only previous physical evidence of crucifixion were bones excavated in Italy and Romania that had holes in the forearms and heels which could have been made during a crucifixion, but no trace of the actual nails that were used to penetrate the body of the victim. One reason for this lack of evidence was that most crucifixions involved the person just being tied onto the cross, with no major loss of blood at the beginning of the ordeal; the death would creep on at a slower pace. The body would still eventually sag in exhaustion until breathing was no longer possible. After death, the distorted body would be dumped into a mass grave.

The first century A.D. of John (and Jesus) was clearly a time of pain, unrest, and turmoil in the ancient Near East. Rome didn't play games. This wasn't a Monty Python movie. When the Jews of Palestine defied their cocky conquerors, with overt gestures of opposition and open acts of rebellion, the Roman response was usually swift and cruel.

Perhaps, because he participated in an uprising, in a cry for freedom, for land, or committed some other grievous offense in the eyes of Rome, John was sentenced quickly to a slow death.

No documents were found that record John's crime or recall his life or crucifixion. All we know is that this healthy, handsome young man was probably taken by soldiers to the outside of the city walls and nailed to a cross; left to hang as a warning and as a living notice of Roman justice.

The nail through his heels that has now made this find famous was preserved by a rare occurrence.

At the time of the crucifixion, after the nails through the forearm of wrists were in place, after the legs were twisted to one side and both heels in alignment, a spike was nailed through both heels into a knot in the hard olivewood cross and the nail bent as it was hammered in.

After he hung for a couple of days, a target for stones and abuse by a city gate, his death was hastened by impatient (or perhaps humane) soldiers when they shattered his legs with a hammer, as his skeletal remains document.

11

Hemorrhaging and shock brought death, but then they couldn't get the nail out of his feet when it came time to take the broken body down. It was wedged in the knot of the olivewood cross.

In one last show of nonrespect for this human being, the Roman guards in charge cut off his feet, removed the rest of the body, and then pried off the whole complex of spike, wooden support plaque, and feet and buried them all along with the rest of the body in a temporary grave.

Soon after, John's remains were disinterred by friends or relatives and removed to their permanent resting place outside the city in a stone casket along with the body of a child of the family. There they remained, in the dust of time, undisturbed, until the metal eartheaters brought them to the light of day in 1968.

From pottery and other artifacts in the tomb, the rough estimate for this Palestinian crucifixion is somewhere between 7 A.D. and 70 A.D. — the exact time and place of Christ.

The cross — a crude instrument of torture and death.

Why do we wear this thing around our necks? The audience in our gospel reading wouldn't wear one; they replied, "Our law tells us the Messiah will live forever, not die on a cross." Some others expected the Messiah to be one who would come in power to overthrow the pagan Roman intruders. Others expected miracles and signs of massive political upheaval and revenge. Jesus wept and suffered and sacrificed.

To proclaim one who has been crucified as the Christ seems an absurd claim. To people working toward power and wealth and status, a crucifixion is a defeat — an unfortunate and unwise predicament to get oneself into.

If one must be executed, at least be like Socrates — very old at the time and then die quickly with some dignity and honor, some sort of euthanasia at least, not on a cross like a criminal.

Paul wrote this to friends in Corinth, Greece:

> *For Jews demand signs and Greeks seek wisdom but*
> *we preach Christ crucified, a stumbling block to Jews*
> *and folly to Gentiles, but to those who are called, both*

*Jews and Greeks, Christ is the power and wisdom of
God.* — 1 Corinthians 1:22-24 (paraphrased)

The cross. The scandal of Christ's cross.

Jesus proclaimed the total worth of all people; he proclaimed unrestricted love — the movement of God; he lived what humanity should be, what humanity was intended to be.

And it went against the flow of society, against all the pseudo-gods and images that people had set up in selfish idolatry.

Christ was a radical correction, going against the flow of self-centered life. From the rough wood manger of a dirty cattle shed, from peasant parents, from rejection by the powerful from an inn-keeper to Herod, it is a life that seems to lead not to victory but to failure ... to a cross. But the story doesn't end in this death.

Even the finality of death, even death on a cross, could not end the power of love, could not push this Christ into the dust of forgotten past. The cross and the resurrection for the Christian mesh into one life view. The cross and the resurrection are woven together.

The cross alone would be just another tragic event in the long history of apparent injustices. Wearing a cross around one's neck then would be a nihilistic, sarcastic statement of hopelessness in a brutal and short existence. Without God's exaltation, Jesus' historical ministry, which ended on a cross, would make Jesus just another Palestinian martyr who died a horrible death, but it would not make this one the Christ.

And the resurrection alone, without the cross, would be just another undetached, questionable story in humanity's quest for God-with-us.

But together, the ministry, the action, the cross, the death, the perceived continued presence, love still alive, together, this takes on the power of something unique; this is transparent to the reality of God; God takes form in freedom and forgiveness, and promises are kept for the future — God takes form in the Palestinian Jew named Jesus.

Christ subjects himself to the ultimate negativities of existence and they are not able to separate him from his unity with God.

This is the Christ — God's Son. An instrument of execution, the cross becomes now the symbol of the greatest show of love at the greatest time of hate. The cross symbolizes that we are in the world of crucifixion but not of that world. There is a purpose and power beyond despair and self-destruction. Divine love is the way of the cross — the cross revealing the nature, the depth, and the sovereignty of divine love. Divine love in our world — sacrificing its own, in extreme humility, even sacrificing itself — this is the nature of this love that gives life. This is what the cross around our necks and on our altars should say to us — struggle, sacrifice, servanthood, and God with us in victory over all forms of hate and separation.

The cross is a symbol of that center of things, that radical correction for the flow of selfishness, the breakthrough of divine love even in the grip of death. It is a symbol of God being active despite our crude forms of hate today — hate and crosses that you and I too often construct — hate molded like a rugged cross to squeeze the life out of others — psychological and emotional crucifixion. Ultimately, both the cross and the grave live, also. We are given forgiveness, direction, and a future.

In the words of Paul:

> *Jews call for miracles, Greeks look for wisdom; but we proclaim Christ — yes, Christ, nailed to the cross; and through this is a stumbling block to Jews and folly to Greeks, yet to those who have heard his call, Jews and Greeks alike, he is the power and wisdom of God.*
> — 1 Corinthians 1:22-24

Holy Cross Day. Amen.

Saint Matthew, Apostle And Evangelist
Ezekiel 2:8—3:11; Ephesians 2:4-10; Matthew 9:9-13

Faithful, Not Successful

Today is a day in the church year that is set aside to remember and commemorate the early church apostle and evangelist, Saint Matthew.

Actually, very little is known about the Matthew mentioned in the Bible as one of the original apostles. But what little is known is quite significant. This gospel reading (Matthew 9:9-13) states that when Jesus asked him to join the movement, Matthew was a tax collector. This in its original historical setting was a radical proclamation of the extent of God's grace and love.

Tax collectors in Palestine were hated people. They were hated not because they reduced people's take-home pay; hated not necessarily because the collectors were allowed to add on a percentage of the take for their own profit, which they did; not necessarily because their collected taxes were in addition to the temple tax collected in each town, which they were. The tax collector was despised with an internal churning hate because of their legal, occupational connection to the local military rule set up by the Roman overlords. Tax collectors were hated outcasts because they were local people who apparently sold out — who compromised their Jewish roots and religion, traditions and law to work for the emperor of Rome, an emperor who bordered on claiming his own divinity. To work for the emperor, to collect his taxes, was to participate in idolatry.

The Word of God through Jesus comes often as a radical rearrangement of things. Jesus ate with tax collectors, ate with sinners, outcasts, not only met with them, talked with them, went to them, but ate with them. Eating together, sharing food, passing around the bread and wine from one hand and mouth to another,

15

reclining at table; this was considered a very intimate act, almost sacred interaction in the ancient Near East. And Jesus ate with outcasts, sinners, and tax collectors-traitors. Jesus not only ate with them but also asked them to join the movement. A tax collector — Matthew — became an apostle.

Remember, too, that Roman tax collectors were successful people, if success is judged in terms of an annual salary. You had to have connections to get that job. Tax collectors lived comfortably in an uncomfortable age.

We are called by God not to be successful but faithful. Matthew accepted a new mission. As we move our way through choosing courses at college, setting priorities and goals and majors and graduate schools, it is perhaps good to remember Matthew. We are called not to be successful in the eyes of the world; we are called to be faithful. Matthew the tax collector becomes an apostle of Jesus, Jesus whom we now call the Christ. A radical rearrangement of the flow of society and definitions of success.

There is an interesting side chapel in France — small, contemporary — that has a simple altar, and on the wall is a painting or series of paintings called the stations of the cross. The artist was Matisse. As you know, I am sure many, if not most, Roman Catholic churches and chapels have somewhere in their naves a series of paintings of statues called the stations of the cross which portray the various stages or stops that tradition has allowed Jesus on his painful walk through the streets of Jerusalem on his way to Calvary.

Well, Matisse, too, painted the stations of the cross. But the Matisse stations of the cross are all out of order. The first station is in a lower row of the painting — the second to the right of it, and a third, but then the next stops are up in the higher row now moving to the left. They weave around in a strange pattern; they seem all wrong, out of order, all different from the way we normally would expect them to be, but that, I think, is the movement of God through Christ — the love and will of God often flows opposite to our normal way of doing things — our normal way of treating people — opposite to the flow of our cultural baggage — running counter to our selfish expressions. God's love and will is often opposite of our definitions of success — our caste systems of racism, sexism, our ways of deciding who are the chosen and who are the outcasts.

Jesus ate with outcasts and chose Matthew, a tax collector, to be an apostle.

Let's jump ahead now to a generation beyond Jesus. The festival day of Saint Matthew has also traditionally been a time to examine the so-called Matthean community in which the gospel that we call the Gospel of Saint Matthew developed.

In the year 70 A.D., in retaliation for an organized Jewish rebellion, Jerusalem was partially leveled by Roman shock troops. The local residents, particularly those who took their religion seriously, were forced to scatter. Included in this group were a number of Greek-speaking Jews who proclaimed Jesus as the Christ. They moved north and settled in a community and formed a church up the coast on the Syrian-Turkish border. More Jews were moving in from the south into this area. Also in this community on the Mediterranean were local Greek-speaking people, some of whom had converted to Christianity, and some of whom kept their local gods.

The newly formed Christian group there felt the need to gather the facts and stories, the tales about this Jesus, the Christ, to share with others in this fast-moving town.

For purposes of worship, teaching, and evangelism, they collected the information about Jesus, some of which, according to tradition, had been written down by the Apostle Matthew. (Tax collectors supposedly were in the habit of keeping detailed records.) Information was gathered from various sources, compiled, and written down around 90 A.D. The gospel, the good news of Jesus, the Christ, our Gospel of Saint Matthew, good news that speaks to the problem of unbelief and like the Matisse paintings of the stations of the cross, the good news often flowed opposite to the pattern of normal human expectations and goals.

It's God's Word. It proclaims the Christ, words of forgiveness and grace that accepts even tax collectors as one of the family, one of the children of a loving concerned parent.

As Christ gave to Matthew a new mission, the Gospel of Matthew proclaims a new mission to that first-century gathering of refugees who were looking for some ultimate meaning in a brutal, confusing age that so often defined success in terms of power and wealth and land. Christ gave them a new mission, a mission that was transparent to the movement of God.

Our goal this morning is not just to understand Saint Matthew, or to understand the Matthean community — what they wrote and why. If we would do just that alone, then we would be good historians, but that's all. Or worse yet, if we took the sacredness of this writing seriously and stopped here, we would make the Bible into some kind of idol.

Our real goal is to go beyond this and ask, "What would Saint Matthew write today if he was among us, in our community? What mission would be given to us?" This is a critical step to remember in your own Bible study. The heart of the matter is to attempt to answer this question.

I think it is a mission that often goes against the flow of things today. It is a mission that calls for us in our totality; it calls for all of us, our whole mind, body, soul, personality, time, place — we, too, are called to be faithful.

This is like that neat surrealistic image where Ezekiel is portrayed as actually eating the scroll that contains God's Word, digesting God's Word and will, making it a part of his very self — incorporating it into his very being. Being grasped by God — this is faith.

We are called to be faithful, and we are sent out. At the origin and the heart of the word mission is the verb meaning "to be sent out."

We are called to be "mission-aries," that's the deepest meaning of our baptism. This is a baptism where God has claimed us as his own, before we were old enough to form illusions about earning our status based on something we did or because we believe certain things.

We have been claimed by God, that's the meaning of baptism; that is the origin of real faith, being grasped by God, and sent out.

We serve, Matthew the tax collector reminds us, not because we want to be saved but because we are saved, chosen.

18

Our Bible study and discussion together should not focus on how we feel about Jesus, but should focus on the question of how God feels about us.

Saint Matthew would remind us that we are part of the church. You can't be a Christian without being part of the church — that cultural, racial mix of people, some of whom we might not like but whom we are called to love, under the blanket of God's forgiveness. We are people who come together for worship, strength, insight, interaction, shared concern, and then are continually sent out in mission.

The church is not a club for saints but a hospital for sinners, where we all have a little of the ex-tax collector in us. Christ did not come to invite virtuous people but sinners — the church is not necessarily made up of those whom you or I happen to like, but the body of those whom God happens to love.

Saint Matthew would say that you are a part of the church and that you cannot know for real that God loves you personally until you meet him at the altar and around his Word.

He sees the church as the suffering servant, the charismatic church. Charismatic means that which contains the gift of the Spirit, the presence and reality of God now and here. Keep in mind, also, that God's Spirit works through non-Christians.

Saint Matthew would say that we must remember that we are catholic Christians. There are many different and valid ways of expression of faith and mission, but when it comes down to the heart of the matter — the church is one under Christ and under one God.

As it has been said to me, "You are a baptized, charismatic, catholic Christian whom God has had his eye on since the foundations of the earth were laid."

Lutheran, Baptist, Episcopalian, and Methodists — all are to be adjectives, not nouns; we are a Lutheran Christian, Baptist Christian, Methodist Christian — Christ is the only base of authority.

Saint Matthew today would say that we have a mission to our world, not the world of the Gospel of Saint Matthew, not a world occupied by Roman soldiers, or the confusion of Greek and Arab mindsets trying to understand one another, but a world today of secularism amid pluralism, all areas of narcissism where the tower of Babel soaring in the sky is constructed out of soda cans from the side of the road, beer cans, sulfur dioxide, nuclear waste, and power politics. It is still a world where poor sinners, twentieth-century tax collectors who have sold out their roots can be picked up from the dust and invited to dinner by Christ himself. It is a world where we are invited to become a part of his movement each day anew, a movement that often flows opposite to values and definitions of success given by the power and status seekers today. It's a movement that often contains stopping places, stations, on a way to a crucifixion, but a movement that through Christ is grounded in the very reality of God, a movement into the promise of love's unending future.

Today is the festival of Saint Matthew, the apostle and evangelist. If we take this character seriously, he is a powerful reminder of our shared mission. Amen.

Saint Michael And All Angels
Revelation 12:7-12; Luke 10:17-20

Angels And Aliens

Like some giant, mystical flock of snow geese stopping momentarily in their fall flight to the south, they are winging at us once again for their annual visit of a few weeks or so before moving on.

I am talking, of course, about angels ... or at least what most of our society envisions as angels today.

I have sighted some earlier this year. They usually don't begin arriving until mid-October, but for the last week or two they have invaded my house, by way of the mailbox. Perched on the front and back covers, and scattered throughout the interior of early Christmas catalogs, were a vast variety of angels.

For example, for $169.95 one can purchase a twelve-piece angel band — handcrafted and hand painted in Italy. There is a little saxophone player, a bassoonist, and a conductor. The catalog calls them "charming and delightful." They wear full-length dresses and smiles and wings. Perhaps an angel tree topper in a flowing gown of gold trimmed in burgundy and beige with a delicately painted porcelain face, could be purchased for $16.95. Or a musical angel, that spins on a stand as she plays "Silent Night" on her harp, costs $15.95.

The angels are coming again for their annual visit, earlier it seems, perhaps more numerous, but just as cute and colorful and symbolically powerless as last year.

Angels have been compared to the last few American bison in our zoos, caged in, swatting flies with their tails — barely representing the mighty herds that once roamed the west. Angels and American buffalo whose numbers and power once shook the earth with thunder, but are now both just tokens — a remnant of a spiritual breed that once was.

There are some indications today that bison are making a modest comeback in some national and state parks and on western cattle ranches; so perhaps there is hope for angels.

I must admit that as a young child, angels were a comforting concept. They were positive and joyful, although you could never pin them down. If they existed, good, and why not? God's world is positive and full of pleasant surprises. But as I got older, I really didn't think much about angels. Maybe what shut them out was the feathers, but all seemed rather foolish, although, I did not think it was proper to consider such endearing religious symbols as foolish. I just didn't think about it. Maybe it was those pink, baroque, naked-male-baby angels — those little chubby cherubs painted by Rubens and others. I didn't have much time for them, never liked them, and their silly, coy smiles. I shut them out.

But as one who haunts the halls of art museums, it is difficult to study historical artwork of any culture — Asian, African, European — without being confronted with representations of angelic creatures that were something other than haunting and engaging, not pink, chubby, or naked; not all down-feathers and hand harps — and yet not fully human either. They were something other — offering by their presence — something other.

During a summer spent in Greece — traipsing through Greek Orthodox churches and museums specializing in the Byzantine era — I consciously wondered again about angels. The angels in the icons were creatures who could see beyond. I now have two copies of angel icons hanging in my office, one of which is Saint Michael peering out the window to the library garden below. If you take the angels represented there seriously, they hold a sense of awe, respect, fear, power, and authority. They are painted as one of us — and yet a stranger — something other.

Our Bible has close to 300 references to angels. I don't think we should ignore angels. If we are sincere in our quest for the meaning of our own personal purpose and how we fit into the very structure of existence, too much of that struggle has already been tied historically into tales of angelic encounters.

The usual Hebrew word for angel means simply "messenger — envoy." Actually the concept of a heavenly messenger is deeply rooted in all the early religions of the Near East as it is in other cultures. Every major Mesopotamian, Hittite, Canaanite, and Egyptian god had his or her messengers who would directly relate to the world and the lives of humanity. Later the Greeks, the far Eastern religions, and the early European mythic, forest tales gathered in the Grimm brothers' collection, all had traditions of messengers from the divine realm who would intersect and change human life. These angels often took different forms — some were even winged. The winged sphinx and griffin and humanoids of ninth-century B.C. Mesopotamian texts, for example, were later called cherubim and seraphim.

Under the Babylonians who captured Judea and Israel, the understanding of angels underwent a profound change. In the Babylonian structure of gods, angels were not merely messengers but were also the controlling spirits of natural phenomena — wind, water, earthquake, and the like.

In our biblical scripture there is no set definition of angels. They play various roles. They appear, they surprise, they announce. They are strangers from beyond. They cannot be pinned down. They come and go freely. In the later apocalyptic writings of the Old Testament like in Daniel, and the books of the intertestamental period like Tobit, Levi, Enoch; and the New Testament book of Revelation, all influenced by Persian symbolic language and concepts, angels are grouped into forces — divided into different ranks and varieties — as vast armies — salvation armies — geared for a final confrontation with "the dark side of the force." The angel leaders were named Gabriel, Raphael, Uriel, and Michael. Michael, for example, chief of the order of virtues, captain of the archangels, prince of the presence — and by decree of Pope Pius XII in 1950 — patron angel of policemen.

In the New Testament, we have messengers — strangers — angels — who come into the story to offer a word that changes a life, and then they are gone. Both ephemeral and mystical, the Pharisees acknowledged angels but the Sadducees denied their existence. And the book of Revelation, as mentioned, offers the Persian concept of angels as the warriors against chaos.

At various times in history, since the New Testament, angels have fascinated theologians. A theologian in the thirteenth century claimed that there were nine choirs of angels, "each choir at 6,666 legions and each legion containing 6,666 angels." I am sure you all calculated that to be 399,920,004 angels in all. But don't worry about an angel population explosion, according to thirteenth-century biblical interpreters, angels are sexless, or at least faithful celibates, with zero population growth set at their creation.

On the other hand, one section of the Hebrew Talmud, a fifth-century encyclopedia of Jewish tradition, ethics, and folklore, stated that new angels are born with every word that God speaks. Another section of the Talmud said that every blade of grass has its angel, which bends over it and whispers to it, "grow, grow." Accordingly, every living organism was created with a guardian angel.

Medieval theologians wrote discourses on nine angelic ranks or choirs — seraphim, cherubim, thrones, dominions, virtues, powers, principalities, archangels, and angels. Using the interlocking, abstract system of cosmology derived from Plato, philosophers divided the universe into nine spheres — each with one of the nine choirs of angels assigned to it. Plain angels assigned to the inner core of the moon and earth (and us), for example: the seraphim assigned to the very principal or force behind the movement of all existence.

When Luther and the Reformation came about, angels were put on the back burner. Luther had nothing against angels and would even defend their existence, but what he also proclaimed was that people could *directly* approach God. One can go directly to the source of all, you need no intermediary, priest or pope, no blessed saints, and no ranks of angels. They were still to hold importance, but now, in the real presence of Christ, God is with us — here — in bread and wine and word. So, for many, all of a sudden, angels were theologically unemployed.

For many Christians they quickly slipped into cupids, or were finished off by rationalism, or are wrapped up with the Christmas tree ornaments most of the year. So why not leave them there? I personally can think of a number of reasons. They are mentioned about 300 times in our Bible. What was their message then? And how does that translate to us today? They often speak good news. Angels have been considered beings that can respond freely to God's love, who are not hampered by our physical limitations and human selfishness. Just for the sake of argument, why can this not be true? I think it is human arrogance to believe that we humans are the climax or ultimate of God's total creation.

To leave open the option of supra-human beings, beyond human, self-realized, love-bearing beings that praise God as the universal Creator, does not to revert back to the Dark Ages. As a civilization that has generated World Wars and now the nuclear blast potential to rend asunder the very fabric of the earth, we have little cause to designate the Middle Ages as dark.

Perhaps as NASA project, Pioneer 10, with its little gold anodized aluminum plaque affixed to its side with a symbol of peace on it and mathematical clues to its origin — all designed for any inhabitants of other worlds who may intercept the satellite — leaves our solar system at 30,558 miles per hour ... and as the 84-foot wide Harvard radio telescope north of Boston listens for hints of life in the depth of outer space — perhaps especially now we can again be humble in the realization of our limited insight into other dimensions. Perhaps we can see more clearly that God is the ruler and prime power within and behind all dimensions and all creations and life forms — even those that may be found to be other than ourselves. In this light, it is safe to say that angels, too, can certainly share in praising God. In this light also, angels remind us that existence has a universal dimension — a universal dimension that is more than just a physical, astronomical universe but also a spiritual universe. The existence of angels suggests the fact that the very fabric of the universe beyond human understanding and sight unites in praise of the one primary force of creative love.

Angels are also reminders that nothing can separate us from the love and presence of God. Historically, as the distance between God and humans increased, angels became more important. In a moment of crushing separation, there was, in a sense, a knock at the door; and a stranger; and the very Word of God was spoken — enacted. Walls of separation crumble when faced with the concept of an angel. Even the wall of death — as a young stranger at a tomb spoke some good news that held — and holds — permanent power. Who was he? A man, a figment of one's imagination, an illusion, or a mythic story figure? But what does it matter if the truth is spoken? Perhaps, they are all real angels.

And, angels can give us some insights into good and evil that wrestles within each of us and the very cosmos. One of the deeper riddles of the biblical record is portrayed in the Revelation story of angels fighting in heaven. How could "blessed spirits" who eternally perceive the divine glory in heaven be so tempted to turn away from God? "Better to reign in hell than serve in heaven," Milton has Satan say.

Let me restate the question in a more personal way. How can we who are given life and the gifts of love turn away from the source of that life and love in pride and prejudice? The very battle between Michael and the dragon is fought not only in the clouds but also within each of us every day. Good and evil are ambiguously interwoven within. In this sense, demons and angels are not spooks in the night but constructive and destructive powers within the very heart and soul of each person and in each of our social groups and historical situations. The Fall of the Angels and the Fall of Adam are mirror images. They are the cosmos and the personal ethical and psychological interacting in the same arena of freedom.

Let us be kind to angels. I like their style and symbol. I like the mystery of it all. We are not alone. Love transcends. I like to be reminded of the vastness of God's intended universe. This is a day to remember that the direction of God's love spells out the final future. We are not in this alone. God does send messengers to us. Chaos does not have the final word — personally or universally.

And our praise of God, our thanksgiving to God is not alone, the very mountains cry out and the sea roars, "Yes," and the creation beyond our comprehension also cries out in praise. It is not just this day that we should be open to angels and share praise with angels, but rather, all time. We share a life of praise to God — the creator of the totality of reality. Amen.

Radically Unfair

In a Walker Percy novel, a white physician is arrested for illegally selling drugs to truck drivers to help them keep awake on long hauls and then put them to sleep after they reach their destination. He is sent to a federal prison for a few months. His prison job is to drive the tractor mower at the eighteen-hole officers' golf club at the adjacent Air Force base.

After this brief prison stay, he returns to his home and his practice in a southeastern state. In the hallway of the local hospital, he is met by a 75-year-old black janitor who gives him this greeting:

"I knowed they couldn't keep you. People talking about trouble. I say, 'No way.' No way Doc going to be in trouble. Ain't no police going to hold Doc for long. People got *too* much respect for Doc! I say."

Well, you don't have to be southern, or African American to understand the subtleties of that brief exchange. In the novel, the physician reflects on the janitor's greeting: "Frank was having a bit of fun with me. And he knew that I knew. He was using the old forms of courtesy to say what he pleased. And what he was pleased to say was: 'So you got caught, didn't you? And you got out sooner than I would have gotten out, didn't you?' Even his pronunciation of police as 'po-lice' was overdone and farcical, a parody of black speech, but a parody he calculated I would recognize." It was a greeting from an old man who must still do manual labor at 75 just to put food on his table but who was still holding on to his dignity. Saying face-to-face, "It's unfair."

Unfair.... What about that parable from the book of Matthew that we read today? Now that is a story which seems to lack in subtleties; portraying an occurrence that is obviously unjust; arbitrary; capricious — downright unfair!

27

The kingdom of heaven is like an estate vineyard owner who went into town at the break of dawn to hire laborers to be paid the standard daily wage — which, at the time of the Roman occupation was one denarius. One denarius would purchase the goods and services to sustain one average-sized family for one day. It would buy sufficient nourishment for the laborer and laborer's dependents (spouse, small children, maybe an elderly grandparent or aunt or uncle no longer able to work). A denarius would buy some food for the day — the basic necessities of life. Nothing could be saved from a day's wage of a denarius, nor could anything extravagant be bought, just sufficient food to maintain physical well-being for the day.

The kingdom of God is like the drama playing out in this vineyard. It was grape harvest time — the time was right — the grapes held the correct amount of ripeness and sugar at the end of growing season, and they had to be picked quickly before a heavy rain could damage the fruit.

When it was this time — the right time for harvest, the owners of vineyards would need additional workers beyond their own maintenance staff, so the owners would go very early in the morning to the marketplace by the community well where poor, unemployed day laborers would gather before sunrise in the desperate hope of being hired for the day. (It was not much different than what occurs today in countless towns and cities in our southwest — designated meeting places for farm laborers who cry out to be hired the day; or in the pine barren towns of central and south New Jersey when the tomato or cranberry crops are ripe — old school buses coming down a dusty lane — needing today perhaps twelve strong backs. "You and you and you and you — get on the bus." Or, there are the migrant workers traveling the central corridor from Ohio to Florida as crops come due, their children in tow. Little hands are also needed to pick the vegetables or fruit. Little hands — needed to get that elusive denarius for the family. Kids in and out of various public school systems; not in any one place long enough to learn how to read. The family staying in run-down motels or seasonal farm barracks; their old pick-up truck constantly breaking down while trying to follow the harvest and hopefully, please dear God, earn a denarius for the day.)

In Palestine at the time of Jesus, the work day for a farm laborer was traditionally twelve hours, from six until six, six days a week. This is another thing that hasn't changed much. In most of what we sometimes call the third world, and that third world within our own world which includes migrant workers, it is still six to six, six days a week. And after the family dinner, paid for with the denarius, it is time to fix the truck, mend the clothes, help with homework, and tend one's own garden plot if fortunate enough to be in one place long enough.

Those who were not hired at first in the parable, those who remained in the market square — killing time — playing cards — were waiting anxiously; desperate as the sun moved high in the sky. When it appeared hopeless for any chance of acquiring a denarius: any chance of acquiring food, health, wholeness — for one's family, then what?

Okay, but for many of us (be honest!) the ending of this parable still seems unfair, doesn't it? I mean those first hired worked *all day* in the vineyard. Why should they receive the same pay as those who worked only a portion of the day, especially those who worked only the last hour out of the twelve? It seems very unfair. We are conditioned to this response.

(It also bothers me when professional football players are paid more for one quarter of a football game than I am paid for a year of work. On the other hand, I am paid more for one week of work than a rural farmer in India is paid for one year of backbreaking work in the fields. I guess that's not very fair, either.)

The parable assumes that the laborers all worked equally hard and the quality of the work was the same, some just worked longer. As the text said, some "bore the day's burden and the heat." The midday sun on Palestinian hillsides before the rainy season can fry both body and mind. Why aren't those who "bore the day's burden and the heat" paid more?

Discrimination as defined by the parable is a very different matter and most often today much more subtle. For example, a comment: "You know, you are one of my good friends. I never

29

think of you as black." Implying what? That I think of you as white and therefore can now accept you because I think of you as being just like me. Or perhaps implying, "I don't think of your race at all — or those other parts of you that are different from me." "Ain't no po-lice going to hold Doc for long." God, as described by the parable, wills the denarius of fulfilling nourishment, which includes unity, for us all.

Those who first heard the parable from the lips of Jesus probably did a better job of hearing the Word in the words, than we often do today. They were listening closely for what this radical rabbi, Jesus, had to say about God. The vineyard was a well-known symbol at the time for the kingdom of God — for the way God intends life to be — for what it is like to be at home with God.

Those who first heard the parable knew the vineyard owner in the story was representing God. For them this was not a confusing story about farm work and working hours. It was about what is fair and what is not fair. What is right in the eyes of God, and what is wrong about the way we often treat each other.

Jesus had been heavily criticized for his contact with so-called "outcasts." He was welcoming, comforting, and healing in his acceptance of tax collectors, widows, lepers, single women, Samaritans, and children. He was heavily criticized. And God, in the parable, asks the critics "are you envious because I am generous? Is the inclusiveness of my love unfair? Or do you not understand the vast extent of my love and my world?"

This is an appropriate parable for us, because it is all about God's driving desire to bring everyone home. That is the kingdom of God — everyone home with God — and in the meantime, making sure that everyone always has at least a denarius in their hand. That's justice. "The kingdom of heaven is like a landowner who went out at dawn to hire laborers for his vineyard." The kingdom of heaven is where everyone always knows your name. Home is where you can always expect to be confronted and forgiven and put under no obligation. Home is where there is always a place for you at the table. Home is also where you can always count on what is being shared on the table.

"Are you envious because I am generous?" asked God through the parable.

This parable of Jesus was especially meaningful to the faith community of Matthew (Matthew is the only gospel that contains this parable) because that Christian community was under heavy verbal attack for welcoming into their fellowship a variety of Gentiles, people with no Jewish-Hebrew background. These new members were very different. In the past, they had worshiped various Greek or Phoenician or other regional deities. They carried different customs and concepts of ancestry. They had different racial connections and worship patterns. But, now they were all united by the acceptance of Jesus as the one who is transparent to God.

"But wait," said some original members of Matthew's fellowship, "do these Gentiles who entered the story at various later hours of the day, do they also get the blessing? Do they get the peace of God, all that one needs to be whole, a denarius of spirit? Can we be blessed by them?"

"Yes!" proclaimed the parable. "Does this seem unfair?" "Do you begrudge my generosity?" asked the owner of the vineyard.

The kingdom of heaven is like a vineyard whose owner is very gracious, giving the unexpected. God desires unity in the midst of sacred diversity and God wills that all receive the denarius: enough food, shelter, health, safety, respect, dignity — a denarius — for everyone waiting in all our marketplaces, life in all its fullness.

God asked, "Are you envious because I am generous?"

Yes. Envious and ashamed. Often in need of your forgiveness, dear God. Often in need of your forgiveness. Amen.

World Communion Sunday
Luke 22:14-17

Unity That Transcends

The World Council of Churches and other interdenominational and international church groupings have set this day aside as "World Communion Sunday."

In the minutes and hours before we gathered here, bread was broken with a blessing and wine and words were shared in other countries and states and towns. At this moment still others are communing, sharing bread and wine and faith defined by Christ. In the minutes and hours immediately after we depart from here, as the earth spins itself open to sunlight west of here, cups will be raised to other lips with the words "my blood shed for you." And, this all seems to me to be very right. A World Communion Sunday!

But is what happens this day so out of the ordinary to the human experience? For example, it is easy to be swept up into the corporate movement of bodies gently pushing against bodies as they pass in the crowded market streets of Amman, Jordan. Let me tell you of a tourist's account:

> *It was warm but comfortable in the early winter evening at the base of a hill that holds the ruins of a Roman amphitheater that looks much the same today as it did 2000 years ago when the Roman Empire stretched to the edge of the Arabian Desert. An amphitheater bathed now in the yellow of artificial flood lights as twilight darkened the sky and the market area enlivened after the workday. It is an Arab market that has the same ambience, I am sure, of the market that was there at the time of the Roman occupation; a swirl of activity, the blend of human voices (speaking Arabic that I do not understand, but it was obvious to me that the voices*

33

held the human communication of greetings and questions and anger and joy); a swirl of color and noise around the spice stands, food venders, cloth merchants, a sidewalk barber, the various butchered parts of camels hanging from twine for close inspection at the meat stalls; and even a moment of our time — a teenaged hawker by a table of pirated Michael Jackson cassette tapes; but a crust of humanity, people close together ... a community.

Yet for me, there was one problem. It was impossible for me to blend in, as I like to do; impossible to blend in and become part of the communion of that community. I was obviously Western, non-Arab; too tall; too pale; my clothes were unmistakably foreign; I had a camera slung over my shoulder. The old market of Amman doesn't have many Western visitors anymore, if it ever did. The few that come to the city now make their business contacts in their hotels out near the airport and then leave quickly. When I was there it was the time when hostages were being taken off the street in Beirut less than 150 miles away, and Israel had just threatened to bomb Amman in retaliation for a West Bank rocket attack that originated in the Jordanian hills. In the crowded market, people stared at me; what was I doing there? They would take a step back from me. By the large open-walled mosque in the market area I was politely but firmly asked to move on — certain that I could not be a Moslem.

In the midst of this vibrant community, I was an outsider — until I found an open seat on the patio of one of the many tiny coffee houses along the market street. You would sit down, and all of a sudden become an honored guest, but more than an honored guest — you would become part of the family of the Arab owner who serves you and part of the family of all those others sipping coffee on the porch. A small glass was presented and perhaps a small, sweet, nut cake, and as the coffee was poured with ancient words of greeting, we were united.

This particular hospitality of incorporation has its roots in the Bedouin past. If you approached the desert tent of a Bedouin family, rich or poor; you would be welcomed, invited in to the shade, to sit together on a rug, your face and hands and feet washed. Then the center of the unity: some flat bread and a glass presented to you, to hold before you as the host pours the potent, black, almost syrupy coffee into your glass from the long curved, graceful lip of an ornate, brass coffee pitcher etched with designs and heated on the rocks of a fir all day, just in case a guest would come. In the desert, it was often a life sustaining necessity, and as you ate and drank together you become family. Even though under different circumstances — in a different location or setting you might be enemies — but when sharing coffee together, there is to be a peace and forgiveness and unity that mirrors the way God (Allah be praised) intended life together to be. And so it is safe to relax and let compliments flow easily and naturally, if only for a few minutes, united, in the sharing of coffee and sweet cake before returning to the imperfection of the swirling daily market gathering.

When the hour came, Jesus took his place at the table with the apostles, and said to them, "I have wanted so much to eat this Passover meal with you before I suffer! For I tell you, I will never eat it until it is given its full meaning in the kingdom of God." Then Jesus took a cup, gave thanks to God and said, "Take this and share it among yourselves...."

Mary Frances Kennedy (M. F. K.) Fisher was, for some, the premiere American writer on food — about eating and what to eat and about people who eat. She was a gifted, creative writer and people would often ask her why she didn't use her fine talent to write about war and peace and love instead of food. In an interview she answered that question by saying: "There is a communion of more than our bodies when bread is broken and wine is drunk."

One could talk about experiences of offered food and hospitality in a poor village in central India, or the offer of bread and salt at a Ukrainian New Year's gathering in a frozen Russian forest, or a

35

Thanksgiving meal at our grandparents' house as a teenager. There is a uniting when eating together in trust and respect and forgiveness, something that contains the spiritual and the universal.

A college senior wrote a paper about the Japanese tea ceremony and included this description, written by a tea master, of what happens when people drink tea together in the ceremony:

First, you sit a moment in a sheltered arbor and enjoy the garden. The play of light and shadow and the rustle of leaves ... you have been invited ... and beckoned by your host, you enter the tearoom through a small low doorway, pausing in an outer room. A few flowers have been arranged for you in a vase. You relax, and then are welcomed into a room with a kettle over a fire and a ceramic water jar and a silk bag encasing a small handmade ceramic tea container. The room is silent save for the water in the kettle that is just rising to a boil. Your host joins you in this world apart and prepares tea for you. Movement anticipates movement, single gestures recede into a continuum; the fragrance of tea fills the room. As if by natural law, a bowl of tea is offered. It is set before you and you bow in thanks to your host. Picking the tea bowl up and placing it on your left palm, you raise it in thanks and after turning it, to observe it; you bring it to your lips.

The first taste of tea is for the eyes. Where the rough glaze of the tea bowl meets the shiny and thick liquid you can see the teachings of nature; water-eroded rock; the moon reflected in a shallow; moss in a rock crevice. This first taste of tea suggests visual images of nature and nature's ever-renewing energy and vitality.

To savor the second taste to the fullest, close your eyes. Sharp, full bodies ... as if you could taste the fragrance of a newly mown field — this is the second taste of tea.

Yet, for all its significance this tasting with the eye and tongue (in fact all that has gone before) is but prologue and preparation for the third taste of tea. The third taste is the climax of the meeting of host and guest, who taste with the spirit and heart. For now the guest at a tea gathering drinks in fully his host's soul. Along with the green powdered tea and hot water the host has added nothing less than his own spirit, his own heart. The gratitude that springs of itself from the heart of the guest is what the guest then shares with the host in return.

Tea tasted in three ways — with the eyes, with the tongue, and with the spirit. The whole of this experience is greater than the sum of the individual tastes. This drinking of tea brings you to the threshold of the understanding that you are not alone in the world, but instead are part of a larger matrix. By drinking tea, you are wed to the others in the tearoom, and to nature, and to your ancestors and descendents. As you proceed in the pursuit of the discipline the taste of tea will change, and when you taste with the spirit, the taste you experience will be the essence of the ceremony.

Do you see some universality in all of this ... something very human seeking a unity that transcends?

Like Jesus in an upper room — sharing all that formed the Passover meal — eating the roasted lamb meat, and the fruit, and the herbs together with close friends, we are remembering past acts of God and then making a promise about the future.

Students in college would understand what I am talking about: It's getting close to midnight, and studying for the test is draining. A pizza is ordered with some mushrooms and sausage and cold cans of Classic Coke. It is time to step aside from this homework stuff of the night routine; and you can smell the pizza coming down the hallway. Heaven knows one doesn't need the food at midnight, but one needs the company together around the bed or table — pulling pieces apart as the cheese stretches — burning one's tongue. You have been invited to this impromptu feast to be yourself with others, and it's okay to talk about what frightens you or what makes you sad or happy, knowing that at that moment around that food with colleagues it is all right to be off guard. You are invited and accepted and special and a guest of a gracious host — sharing intimacy along with the food — intimacy!

Could all this desire for communion — for union — be tied into the intent of this day, World Communion Sunday? Could the intent be sharing bread and wine in this place of gathering now — here? Here, too, the offered hospitality, the acceptance, the forgiveness, the will for harmony and life giving sustenance is where physical and emotional and spiritual needs can be fulfilled by the grace of God.

Could it be that the Christ who is present here with us, that we confess this morning, defines all the other expressions of human unity where acceptance, forgiveness, and love are genuinely merged with food and drink?

Can one see the power of these universal moments because they are God-originated, containing the very presence of Christ?

God seems so conceptual at times — so theoretical, but when we are here together to share bread and wine and gospel, we have an image of the future unity. Unity, here now again in bread and wine and word for us to share with all our brothers and sisters around the globe this day. All sealed with a promise that this meal is obviously right and intimate and is a touch of the kingdom — the feel of loving eternity. The gracious host is God! The gift contains resurrection. Christ is present!

Around our table, he took some bread and wine and gave it to us saying, "Take and eat, and drink, this is my body and my blood — given for you and for all people, out of love — offered for you forever."

Praise be to God! Amen.

Reformation Day
John 8:31-36; Romans 3:19-28

The Radiating Reformation

The assigned lesson reading from Romans for this festival worship includes these comments by Saint Paul, words that strike to the heart of the Reformation.

> *... The righteousness of God (the final unity for us) has been manifested ... the righteousness of God through faith in Jesus Christ for all who believe. For there is no distinction among us, since all of us have sinned and all of us fall short of the glory of God, we are justified. We are made whole by God's grace as a gift through the redemption which is in Christ Jesus ... which is received by faith.* — Romans 3:22-25 cf

And then our reading from the gospel stated it again. In a less complicated form, Jesus said, "If you continue in my word, you are truly my disciples, and you will know the truth, and the truth will make you free ... (and) ... if the Son makes you free, you will be free indeed."

The Reformation was and is, at its best, a call to all those in the Christian family to center in, to closely examine their own person-hood which includes their own involvement in the greater way of life that helps to form them. To center in and ask oneself, "How do my hopes and fears, my guilt and anxiety and selfishness, and my times of joy and mellowness, and pleasure and my desires, and study, and occupation, and servanthood, and my sense of home and future ... how does all of this, all of me, engage with the will and way of God?" When and why am I a love-bearing being, and when and why am I less than godlike? When does my

39

expressed personhood pull others and me down into moments of darkness and separation — fragmented? And what offers us grounded hope?

Part of the intent of this service of worship is to be so bold as to attempt to capture the message of the Reformation. It is to celebrate our unity as Christians, and to share the very real presence of Christ offered to us through even the material gifts of our ordinary, shared life together, such as through gifts of water, wine, and bread. All this is merged with the Word and therefore bearing love and future promises.

I thought it would be appropriate to include in these comments a brief historical review of the Reformation events, emphasizing causes and purposes. Rather than conjuring up images of old Wittenberg, Luther, Melanchthon, the 95 Theses, Edward the VI, the 39 Articles, and Cranmer's Bible-based *Bible Book of Common Prayer*, want to reinforce that the celebration of Reformation is not based on remembrances alone. After all, the Reformation was, and is, a dynamic process and a current challenge.

Rather than attempt to reconstruct the shadow contexts and contents of history, I have decided instead to begin with a review of the origins of the Reformation. Instead of using Luther or Elizabeth's theologians, let's update it all with something more upbeat and contemporary. I have decided to tell you instead about Squat Theater in New York City, which also is reformational.

Squat is a theatrical group from Budapest that has been living and working in New York since 1977. The group still performs its plays in a converted storefront theater on West 23rd Street near Eighth Avenue called The Building.

I am not sure how to describe the style of their drama. I guess you could call it contemporary. One might be tempted to say "realistic," though it avoids conventional "realism" by using definitely unrealistic images. In the play, *Mr. Dead and Mrs. Free*, there is a twelve-foot papier-mâché baby center stage. It is a colossal baby wearing stereo headphones, its eyes replaced by television screens. The "realism" here is in the play's comments about an acoustically and mass media-stoned youth culture. Here is the sharp tongue of realism. But more!

In artistic terms it is taking a step beyond realism because it attempts to step into your personal space; which, of course, is what the Reformation did.

The theater group's original hope was to mesh art form and real life. They wanted to find a solution to one of the contemporary theater's most vexing dilemmas — the fear — that real, authentic, day-to-day modern life itself might be more dramatic and theatrical and certainly more dangerous than anything one might experience in theater. The dilemma becomes how to infuse theatrical drama with a sense of the real energy and experience of the daily drama of life. Or to put it another way — how to prevent the theater from becoming an escape from the lessons and insights and responsibilities that may spring from the intensity of daily life.

The Reformation, after all, included the call to enter daily the fray of life, seeing Christianity not as an escape from personal responsibility but a call to you personally to live your priesthood, to live your sainthood, to bring God's Word into the middle of things.

Squat works and acts as a collective, sharing profits and debts among the troop. The program credit for its productions read simply, "... written, produced, and directed by Squat Theater." Equality and equity at the heart of our unity is not just revolutional language but also reformational language. Equality and equity is at the heart of our unity.

Being prophetic is part of this call! Squat was prohibited from performing in public after their first performance in their home country. Hungarian government censors considered them to be too explicit and too relevant. They were accused of creating artwork that was, according to the censors, obscene and "likely to be misinterpreted from a political point of view."

The Reformation demanded that the church be explicit and relevant and the powers-that-be tried to close them down.

Is the articulation of the gospel message through our lips and actions today explicit and relevant and faithful? Is it prophetic? The Reformation calls us to be prophetic, which includes challenging the intention of our surrounding organizations and systems if they seem to sway from servanthood and justice, or your church, if it sways from its Christocentric purpose for being.

41

Squat wants to let the "real world" enter into their productions. So at the 23rd Street theater, a black curtain is yanked open near the beginning of each production revealing a large glass wall and glass door facing the street, so the random, unpredictable ebb and flow of street life enters into the productions. People of all descriptions look through the glass, some pressing their faces up against it, looking not only at the actors but also at the audience who now becomes a part of the drama along with the street people. No elitism or escapism allowed here!

In one play, a jeep drives up to the window and a group of soldiers carrying a bloody, wounded comrade storm into the theater through the door and train their guns on the audience, as the jeep drives back into the street and blends into the real traffic, disappearing into the night lights.

Sometimes it is hard to know what is intended and what is unintended. One night someone passing by the theater mistook a fictional shooting for a real shooting and called the police, who stormed into the theater with guns drawn on the audience — this time real guns.

This is a drama group trying to be reformational in the sense of bringing truth into the realm of theater. Not quite pulling it off, of course, but attempting again and again with new productions to speak to the needs and questions of the moment. Is that not the call of Reformation to the church and to us?

Squat was attempting to replace the comfortable structure of the theater with the threatening unpredictability of real life. The Reformation was attempting to replace the insulating structure of the church with the will to allow divine love to flow into the unpredictability of real life ... to mend together the Word and the world ... to sew together the context and content of the gospel.

Reformation was and is based, I believe, on God's will that the community of faith is always to be engaged in renewal and reform, attempting in each new moment to drive love into expressions of justice and peace, compassion and unity.

What would we as Christians, individually and in community, offer others? The Reformation said, "Let's begin at the center."

Our expression of faith should be a Christocentric expression of faith, hope, and love. Christ at the core. Therefore, it must be scripturally centered in continuity with Luther's Christ- and gospel-centered "canon within the canon." If one views Jesus Christ as the center point of the manifestation of love, then the old Reformational axiom, "the finite is capable of the infinite," is true and all our sacred personalities hold the possibility and potential, in each moment, of sainthood even in the midst of our less than loving expressions of separation.

But the core is still the promise that nothing can separate us from the offer of eternal love. A promise of Christ present. A word that allows even water, bread, and wine to hold and speak of eternity.

In the light of the Reformation, servanthood, self-giving compassion, sacramental worship, scriptural study, and an analysis of contemporary life through the eyes of faith are the supporting structure of our ministry together as Christians.

But it is not these actions and intentions that form us as the Catholic, Evangelical church — the Spirit-led, one church that transcends denominational lines. Rather it is only the gift and presence of the Christ given for you.

Now is the time of reformation. Now, when our political structures desperately need skilled peacemakers, when our environment is being abused and needs harmony, when vast sections of our human family are in need of physical healing and the release from hunger. Now, when rich and poor people are crushed by a sense of meaninglessness there is the need for reformation, and for faithful servants through whom the Word of God can work.

There is freedom in this risk and responsibility because the center gift is freely offered. "For it is by God's grace that you have been saved through faith. It is not a result of your own efforts, but God's gift."

One's deeds alone cannot entice or remove God's love. God wills unity and peace and offers the gift of grace. The Easter word is that even death cannot break the unity. The grasp of God's love holds the process of eternity. It is the "Yes" that can only finally transcend all the "Nos" that radiate from our fragile existence.

43

God's kind grasp is a loving, eternal unity, a divine Easter promise that offers now and always to lead us from darkness into light, from self-destruction into the wholeness of healing servanthood. It is a loving grasp that also will not — perhaps by nature *cannot* — let go.

Paul wrote, "There is no distinction among us, since we have all sinned and fallen short of the glory of God. Our justification, our being made right with God, is a free gift of divine grace ... offered to us — observed clearly through the eyes of faith in the suffering, death, and resurrection of Jesus Christ."

There are many reformational reminders for us — but they all radiate from that center promise that is held gently before us in the words and the will of Jesus: "Be not afraid"; be not afraid of any other authority: governmental, educational, societal, ecclesiastical power, or structure. Be not afraid of any emotional or physical or psychological attempt to pull you down to something less than you were intended to be. "Be not afraid" ... "for if the Son makes you free, you will be free indeed." Amen.

Psalm 46 And Reformation Today

Chaos breaking into life, from creation to now — today's psalmody was Psalm 46. The reason this psalm was chosen for Reformation Sunday is because this psalm was what inspired Martin Luther in the year 1529 to write his most famous hymn, "A Mighty Fortress Is Our God." It is a hymn that soon became a symbol of the Reformation and a creed, a statement of belief for the Protestant church and more recently for the whole Western church.

Historians are not sure of the exact context, the exact historical background from which the original Psalm 46 evolved. A few guess that the poem or psalm was inspired by the deliverance of the holy city of Jerusalem from the invading armies of Sennacherib, king of the neo-Assyrian empire in the eighth century B.C.

The inhabitants of Jerusalem were given new life when Sennacherib moved his armies elsewhere, so in this hymn, Psalm 46, with renewed hope they looked at the full meaning of their life in relationship to God.

Other historians connect the psalm with the chaotic times of the third century B.C. It was a time of senseless destruction and agony because of the wars throughout the Near East brought about by the struggle for power among the successors of Alexander the Great. After his death, Alexander's commander and advisors fought for control of his vast empire. In this crisis, the people of Israel looked for some meaning and they found an answer in Psalm 46.

I believe the psalm was used in both these times and that the actual origins of the psalm are much older. Its use of vocabulary and style seem to point to a time before the eighth century B.C. The allusion to wars, the roaring of nations, and tottering of kingdoms seem to be too general for particular reference. It's more of a general statement about life in the passage of time.

45

I agree with the theory that suggests Psalm 46 was originally a hymn for use in the important religious New Year's Festival. It was a time when the new crops were planted, and the people celebrated God's triumph at the time of creation over the forces of chaos.

The New Year's Festival celebrated this triumphant victory for them at the present time, and for all time to come. Psalm 46 offered renewed meaning to the Israelites in the eighth century and the third century B.C., and to Martin Luther in the sixteenth century and I think it has something important to say to us today. The psalm is divided into three sections and each section presents a pattern in the movement of time.

The first section speaks of the chaos in nature that was there from the beginning of creation. The second section talks of the present chaos in life now — the chaos evoked by worldly powers and by people. The third section is about the promise of God for the future — that his ultimate intent for life is for wholeness and peace. The general theme that pervades the entire psalm is the faith that God is near at all times and gives us the strength to face the chaos that constantly threatens to break into our lives.

Let's look now at each section. The first section gives us an interesting picture of early man's view of creation. They believed that in the beginning was chaos — swirling water — gases — with no purpose. God separated the waters and made mountains to hold up the sky — mountains as the foundations of the world — and then he brought life to the world. Life that was good. God the Creator brought purpose, direction and has promised this to his people, even in the times when chaos seems to once again break into our lives.

Let's read the first section again:

> *God is our refuge and strength, an ever-present help in*
> *trouble. Therefore we will not fear, though the earth*
> *should change, though the mountains shake in the heart*
> *of the sea, though its waters roar and foam, though the*
> *mountains tremble at its surging.*   — Psalm 46:1-3

46

The psalm proclaims that at the time of the creation, God showed that he was mightier than the monsters of chaos and established forever his direction and dominion over the world.

Therefore we should not fear that the earth should change or even be dissolved. Though the foundations of our world totter and quake before the rearing, crashing, seething waters of meaninglessness which threaten to submerge our ordered lives and reestablish the reign of chaos; though natural and nuclear holocausts threaten to melt even the rocks, we will not fear because the Lord of hosts is with us. The Lord of creation is in our midst and we are now witnessing some of the worst imaginable catastrophes in the physical world. And more than that, the second section proclaims that the Lord is also the one who offers meaning to all the people of the earth even in the midst of nations and people that roar for war and kingdoms that surge in attack and explode in hate.

The second section reads:

> *There is a river that brings joy to the city of God, to the sacred house of the Most High. God is in that city, and it will never be destroyed; at early dawn he will come to its aid. Though nations are in turmoil, kingdoms totter, his voice resounds, the earth melts away — the Lord of hosts is with us; our stronghold is the God of Jacob.*
> — Psalm 46:4-7

God, our refuge and defense — *ein feste burg* — a mighty fortress. He has well proven himself to be a very present help in trouble since ancient times. The warring, the hatred, the hostility of others cannot separate us from the power of life.

The psalmist then ends his poem and confession by envisioning the final purpose for us in God's plan. He tries to envision wholeness and peace — a time without war or hatred or chaos.

Section three looks at a personal future:

> *Come and see what the Lord has done. See what amazing things he has done on earth. He stops wars to the end of the earth, he breaks bows, splinters spears and sets shields on fire. "Stop fighting," he says, "and know*

47

that I am God, supreme among the nations, supreme over the world." The Almighty is with us — the God of Jacob is our fortress. — Psalm 46:8-11

This is Psalm 46 — a confession of intense faith, a realization that nothing can separate us from the love of God. It is a statement of belief by a person and a people that even in the face of meaninglessness, chaos, war, and distortion, God's will of love reigns supreme. It was a confession of belief that Luther adopted as his own in his hymn, "A Mighty Fortress Is Our God." Luther's primary addition to this psalm was to say that Jesus Christ is the one who clearly defines this all-powerful God of continuing creation.

The psalm and hymn became a symbol of the Reformation. The Reformation was really a call to reevaluate one's relationship to God the Creator — reevaluate how one's life, one's hopes and fears, one's guilt, one's concerns, how one fits in with the power and direction of all life.

The Reformation asked if Christianity was affecting you on this personal level. Does it give strength and meaning to you even in the face of chaos? In October of 1517, Luther's 95 Theses were not a declaration of war against a denomination but rather an assertion that we must be open and receptive to the workings of the creative Spirit of God now in our daily lives.

Chaos is separation from God's plan of love. Where is there chaos breaking in today? Where is there need of reform today?

I read a short story written by a person who grew up in the rural midwest and who found signs of chaos and need of reform in his hometown churches. Outwardly there appeared to be peace and harmony. In his youth he was a member of one of the 63 different churches in his small county. The churches seemed to treat fellowship and friendship seriously. The people said table grace before meals, the children said their bedtime prayers, and they participated in individual and group Bible studies. Everyone attended baccalaureate services; there were popular quilting parties and potluck suppers. But on closer inspection, there was evidence of chaos breaking into the picture, disorder, and evil welling up in the soul of this life.

The children said their prayers but also included racial slurs in their school yard play. The people studied scripture verses on love of neighbor, but there was also a wrong side of the tracks in the town — a division of class — the foundations of love were shaken. There was always a good turnout for the visiting missionary but people wanted little of their church pledges to go to world missions; everyone knew everyone else but forgiveness was often slow in coming.

It was people — the church in need of reform. Some of those needs for reform, I am sure, are valid for us also. But in many other ways, our situation is very different than that picture of the rural midwest. We live in an area and time where it seems that the majority of our neighbors sleep in on Sunday morning, or where time is planned around schedules and not worship; where the local band director can say, "If you want to go to church, you can quit the band" — and a time and place where the Christians are very unsure of themselves. There is a loss of confidence not only about faith but also about our self and our purpose. People today easily slip into despair. Marriages and family life today seem so shaky and fragile. The Christians tend to keep their faith to themselves. They are often embarrassed to share it. We often don't have a vision of personal mission, sometimes even to our children. We have lost the concept of the home as the primary place of Christian education.

Signs of chaos breaking into our life and world can easily be seen around us, and we fear chaos more readily today. We have lost some of our confidence in God as a Mighty Fortress — as the continuing God of creation in our lives now — always creating and victorious over chaos.

Now is the time for reform. Reformation Sunday was never a celebration of a division in the church that occurred in 1500, but Reformation Sunday is a celebration of renewal and a day to recall the revolutionary, reforming, Word of God. It is a time of promise pointing to the power of God, of this movement toward wholeness for all life. It is a day that reminds the church of the provisional nature of all that is less than God.

Reformation was not a once-for-all event but rather it is a permanent state of the church. We are to be the reformers today — we are the instruments of God's Word and we can't afford to play games with that kind of responsibility. Now as always is the age of the Reformation. The God we proclaim has the power to be our ultimate refuge and our strength — an ever-present help in distress. Though the foundations of existence shake, though nations and people are in turmoil, and kingdoms totter — the Lord Almighty is with us. The God of Jacob is our refuge. He is our mighty fortress. Now as always is the Age of the Reformation and we must be the instruments of reform.

May the peace of God, which passes all understanding, keep our hearts and minds through Jesus Christ. Amen.

Allowing Your Sainthood To Surface

Today we celebrate All Saints — historically a major festival in the church year — celebrated internationally, and across denominational boundaries. It is a victory party for those who share in resurrection eternity.

For example, today's reading poetically portrays the total picture. It is from the closing chapters of the book of Revelation to John. The author was one of the leaders, a pastor, of a number of churches in Asia Minor (in Turkey) at the close of the first century A.D.

These churches were under intense persecution from the authorities of the Roman Empire. It was the first really major, across the board, organized persecution from Rome that had a severe impact on most Christian fellowships. Domitian was the emperor, and supposedly to unify his regional governors, he enforced the cult of emperor worship.

All citizens and inhabitants had to publicly worship and be officially recorded offering a sacrifice to the emperor.

The governors in Turkey, more so than anywhere else, strictly enforced the decree. Most people could live with the requirement and viewed the requirement as just another bureaucratic inconvenience like an additional sales tax.

Some considered it a civic responsibility like jury duty — nothing more. After all, one could still officially sacrifice to the emperor with a smirk, a sarcastic reverence, and then go home and worship the gods of one's own choice.

But Christians saw the demand as a matter of faith and conscience. There is but one God — defined and revealed by the Christ. To play the game of emperor worship would be apostasy and idolatry, hypocrisy and heresy — it would be selling out one's soul.

51

For that position of faith, the Christians in Asia Minor at the time of Domitian paid the price in confiscated goods, lost jobs, physical abuse, banishment, separation of family members, and even execution.

The author of Revelation (the church leader John) for example, was banished to a prison island in the Aegean. It was there on Patmos that he told his poetic, sweeping vision of time and history.

History, for John, is a theatrical drama — and the entire world is a stage — or at least the entire world that he knew, which was the Roman Empire. In the script, the church was in mortal combat against the pagan political powers of the time — Domitian and Rome.

Behind the drama and interaction of these characters was yet another drama — the real drama. Heaven and hell are in action. It is cosmic war between Satan and God.

The characters have been transformed, altered. Rome is Satan. The Emperor Domitian is the beast, the dragon (and probably many of the other fantastic images used by John). The faithful Christian believers, the saints, and the church, the bride of the Lamb — these are seemingly overpowered by the muscle, the throw-weight, the military supremacy of Rome.

But the saints, according to the script, according to John's big picture, will be ultimately victorious because the saint is in union with God through Christ the Lamb. The apparently helpless sacrificial Lamb is victorious over the powerful jaws of the dragon because the Lamb is of the eternal God. After the final, conclusive defeat of evil, the martyred saints will be (according to John's revelation) in union, in eternal fellowship with God.

Today's reading is the very poetic vision of that end time. It is a neat attempt, I think, to describe that which cannot be described — personal union with God beyond our dimensions; a heaven; a place; a spaceless location where the saints are united; a place of light containing no darkness of separation; a total movement in a state of love; the faithful ones in eternal fellowship with God.

Quite frankly, some don't think the book of Revelation holds a lot of new insights into God or into the future for that matter.

The symbolic language and sacred numbers and formulas that riddle the book speak to and about the first and second century, but the big picture of good and evil and the ultimate victory of God and the reunion of the saints, as poetically painted by John, is right on target and a glorious vision for celebration on All Saints or any day.

But let's now attempt to draw ourselves into the picture. A campus pastor asked students in a discussion class the question, "What is a saint?"

And there seemed to be a consensus on two characteristics.

First, a saint was one who has a firm belief in God, one who has a faith relationship with God through Christ. Other people can see God's will reflected through the words and actions of these individuals.

The second criterion for a saint, mentioned by most of the group, was that the saint is one who suffers persecution for the faith.

That dual description fits in with the origin of the day. In the year 609, the pantheon in Rome was decreed a Christian church, remodeled and dedicated to Saint Mary and all martyrs.

In the year 741, on November 10, Pope Gregory III dedicated a chapel in old St. Peter's basilica in Rome to "all the saints." In 835, Pope Gregory IV made November 1, All Saints' Day in the Western church. The grip of Domitian was broken, though, of course, none in their right mind would call this new time of civil support for the church the luminous heaven described by John, but a day was set aside to commemorate the martyred saints.

He asked the students in the group to name some saints. They came up with a parade of first-century characters — gospel writers, disciples, and a few names from those first few centuries in the life of the church, like Saint Francis. Then at least one person named some saints much closer to us in time, Mother Teresa, or Martin Luther King, Jr.

They began to wonder if they knew any saints personally. Look again at the criteria they had set: those living their faith in Jesus Christ — those persecuted for their Christian lifestyle.

One way to perhaps grasp hold of this concept of *saint* and have some real ownership of it would be to pick a saint and examine her life or his life, then see what makes her/him tick. Or because I like doing things a little differently, reverse the process, and pick a character that is or was definitely not a saint and examine the components of that life to help us discover clues as to what constitutes a saintly life or a demonic life.

Perhaps the best non-saint to dissect is that character which the author of Revelation singled out to be the personification of the devil — Domitian — the beast, the dragon, the anti-Christ — Titus Flavius Domitianus, son of Vespasian, successor of his older brother, Titus. His last years were known as a reign of terror. He combined suspicion and pride into a deadly combination, killing off potential challengers.

He filled the capitol with statues of himself, announced the divinity of his father, his brother, his wife and sisters, as well as his own divinity. He required officials to speak of him as *Dominus et Deus noster* — our Lord and our God. All citizens were to worship him. Uncompromising Christians were severely punished. Domitian went mad out of suspicion and hate. His wife and a handful of servants stabbed him to death at the age of 45, in the fifteenth year of his reign, in 96 A.D., the beast, the dragon — Domitian.

Look deeper into the record with me. In one book, it was curiously noted that Domitian was efficient in making major reforms in morals and religion. Knowing that historians are often far from objective, particularly imperial historians, I dug a little deeper into the life and the times of Domitian.

I found that the devil had another side. As a young ruler, in his first decade, Domitian was surprisingly competent and just. He enforced the Julian laws against adultery, tried to put an end to child prostitution, forbade indecent public theatrical (pantomime) performances, put an end to the practice of castration, which had spread, with the rising price of eunuch slaves. He refused bribes and he honestly attempted to reduce graft in his government.

The Christian community would have supported him in all these acts of justice, but as the years went by, the pressures of the job, the threats, the temptations, the confusion of his childhood, his deadly marriage, the power, and the dark side of his human personality began to regularly surface, dominate, and take control, even to the point of him proclaiming himself as the power of life — as God.

Domitian was all too human, because he gave up his humanity. Though made in the image of God, he tried to reconstruct himself in his own image separate from God. It was this part of Domitian that was used by John as a picture of pure evil.

As Christians, we all have a bit of sainthood in us and a bit of Domitian. A saint is a person who has been intersected by Christ, grasped by God, and who allows God's love to take the form of personal action, love in action, which the saint knows is grounded in the authority of God.

I think that traditionally on All Saints' Day we have tended to look too deeply into the past to find our saints or perhaps have looked too far away from home. Today I would like us to look within.

A saint is one who has been intersected by Christ and is in a faith relationship, which perhaps we cannot define or pin down, but a faith exists despite our doubts. That probably describes you!

A saint is one in which God's will is obvious in one's actions. When you allow the love of God to surface in your life, in your interaction with others, you are meeting the qualifications of a saint.

Those actions, by nature, will often flow against popular opinion, peer pressure, accepted behavior, and the prudent man economic theory. Those actions flow against persecution in many subtle, and not so subtle forms, and will drive you into the last category of sainthood — one who is persecuted for the faith.

But before we get too satisfied with ourselves, let's put all this into perspective, because I know you and I know myself all too well, and there is also a lot of Domitian in us all. We are a most glorious and motley mix of saint and sinner — children of God; halo and cloven feet but always under the umbrella of God's love and grace, and in need of his gift of bread and wine.

We are called to allow our sainthood to dominate our lives — to allow our sainthood to break the surface of our relationships in loving interaction more times than not.

In other words, All Saints is our day — a day to celebrate and share with Christians past and present. It is a day where no boundaries are valid. It is resurrection now. Time, space, racial, cultural, regional, and economic distinctions hold no power. All Saints is a Christian claim that in communion today around the world, we have a taste of that luminous new city of God proclaimed by the author of the book of Revelation — Christians together called to allow our sainthood to surface.

It is All Saints' Day — our day. Amen.

Dead, Deified, Or Different?

Blest are the lowly; they shall inherit the land. Blest are they who hunger and thirst for holiness; blest are they who show mercy; blest are the peacemakers.

As you are all aware, today is All Saints' Sunday. In the year 835 A.D., Pope Gregory IV established for the Western church November 1 as All Saints' Day.... The Sunday following became All Saints' Sunday.

The day was intended to be a day of celebration and commemoration of all the saints of God, known and unknown — a victory party for those who shared in the mystery, yet continuity, of resurrection eternity.

Unfortunately it is hard for many of us today to get into the party mood because saints seem so distant — so removed from the action of our daily living. The whole theme of "All Saints' Day" seems to take on a rather musty air like something experienced when peering into a dusty corner in the attic of history.

Saints are from a different time of self-perception; a fascinating topic in the realm of church history, but are they really relevant to the bottom line of our daily interaction?

I asked a study group of students once to define "saint" and then to name some saints. Their definitions and candidates all seemed to fall into one or more of three categories: "A saint is someone who is either deified, dead, or different."

First there were those saints who are practically deified. From the ancient stories about them, they seem pretty godlike in total personality. We envision them with halos. They are the superstars of past ecclesiastical piety. You can easily tell who they are because "saint" seems to be a part of their name. Saint John, Saint

Mark, Saint Augustine, Saint Francis — yet also all are apparently removed from us by a large slab of time.

And all the saints that were listed by the students in my study group, except for one, were dead. They were people in the past who had died in the faith, and in most cases died for the faith due to intense persecution. This was important for canonization by my study group — Saint Stephen and Saint Peter — and listed here were more modern names — like Dietrich Bonhoeffer — a young pastor and theologian who was executed by the Nazis toward the end of World War II — saints as people who had put their bodies on the line for their faith and were killed.

Then there was the third category. The students agreed that saints were willing to go against the people that are faithfully different. Saints were willing to go against the flow of the ordinary, to risk and sacrifice their lives for their faith. In our initial discussion, it was in this category that the students placed the one, contemporary saint that was a part of their list: Mother Teresa. Mother Teresa was a little, fragile woman living out her life as a part of a religious order serving in the city slums of India and other parts of our world where human need and desperation seem to peak.

In the eyes of our society, she was a very different kind of person — a woman who, it appeared to the world, had sacrificed what most people seem to define as pleasure and comfort and success so that she could minister to those who are most obviously in physical need. Her ministry was in the very style of Jesus Christ. She was a woman who had forsaken a biological family and personal safety and any kind of possessions. She was a woman who fasted, wore a habit, spent hours in prayer — a person who was very different — like Saint Francis caring for the birds and talking to the birds.

Respected, revered — Mother Teresa won the Nobel Peace Prize. A contemporary at that time, but it appears to us she was someone who was very different from us.

Well the odds are good, of course, that all the people, represented by the names that I mentioned, were or are saints of God.

But deified? These people were lifted up in our memory, in most cases, because some of their actions were godlike, or more specific in human interrelational terms, Christlike. But if we study the record closely, we quickly discover that they are also human creatures of limitation and separation — just like us.

Many are certainly dead, but let's also look around — in our very midst. Yes, saints are always different, in the sense of living a faith that results in actions and philosophies that often fly in the face of societal expectations that are based on ego or self-interest. When the will of God acts through a person, that person, now a saint, becomes in that very moment a divine corrective to loveless action and momentum.

Let me describe to you some "different" people that were encountered during a chapel field trip to Chicago some time ago. It was different in the sense of being saintlike.

The first person I'll describe is Dan Jorenko who works for the Northwest Community Organization — a neighborhood action-justice organization in a low-income neighborhood of active shops and stores. All the signage there was in Spanish. Most of the people on the street seemed to be Mexican or Central American.

It was about noon when we arrived in this neighborhood. I went into the storefront office to find Dan. The front office had the feel of a Dickensian sweatshop for accountants. There were five or six ancient wooden desks buried under a sea of papers. I found Dan in the back room, his hands covered with ink, cranking out flyers on an old mimeograph machine. The flyers were about a neighborhood meeting at St. Mark's parish hall — a meeting to help convince city officials of the need for low-income apartments in the neighborhood, places to live that are rehabilitated and sanitary. There were many families desperately seeking a place to live. One side of the flyer was in Spanish, the other side in English. At the bottom it said, "For a ride ... call Dan at NCO."

We went to lunch at Arandas Cafe at the corner of the block to talk. Over Mexican sausage sandwiches and enchiladas (ask Jeff about beef brain burritos) we tried to talk. That was somewhat of a mistake because this was an authentic Mexican cafe and the music was blasting away — so maybe only six or so of us could actually hear Dan.

Dan told of political wars that were trying to bring about justice in his little area of the city. They were getting very poor people to see that they, too, have rights; trying to build a sense of dignity in people who for the most part felt that they had been forgotten by the normal process of goods and services. Dan was a graduate of Michigan State and then a Methodist seminary. He decided not to seek a call as a pastor of a church because he was afraid that he would *not* be placed in a poor section of the inner city.

Almost three years prior to our meeting, he took this poor paying job with NCO, living in an old apartment two blocks from the office. He works days and most nights. Wearing a torn shirt and ripped jacket, holding a burrito in ink-stained hands, he talked about how he cared for people. He had a certain smile and a sparkle in his eyes, and could see only the positive things that were happening around him, even when his stories seemed to all be about uphill battles against forces of prejudice and apathy, which were affecting families in desperate need. Dan kept a spark of hope and joy in the midst of all this. It was a part of his faith. Is this a saint, perhaps?

Blest are they who show mercy; blest are the single-hearted for they shall see God. Blest are you when they insult you and persecute you and utter every kind of slander against you because of me.

During the same trip, we talked to Gary Mills at St. Mary's Lutheran Church. It's a mission church in the basement of a low-rent apartment house now owned by the American Lutheran Church. The pastor's parsonage is across the street — that street and the few blocks around it have the highest homicide rate in the United States. It seemed like a nice enough neighborhood, but the year prior to our visit, about 48 children between the ages of eleven and 21 were knifed or shot to death there. We watched a videotape in the parsonage basement Sunday morning about the mission's neighborhood and ministry.

For what seemed, to me, to be forever, it showed a string of wallet-size school pictures of boys — giving that school-picture smile like they must have promised their mothers. They were all children that were killed the previous year in gang assassinations on the street outside of St. Mary's. Gary told of one funeral for an eleven-year-old where a rival gang with guns drawn stormed into the funeral service, pushed the bereaving family aside, knocked Gary to the floor, took the body of the slain boy out of the casket, carried it out into the street, and threw it on the top of a car. These were desperate teenagers trying to steal everything from their enemies — even hope. To them there was no meaning to anything — even the words of the funeral or the tears of a dead child's mother.

We slept that night in an office that had a bullet hole through the window, the bullet lodged in the wall. We worshiped that next morning in the boiler room, which doubles as their sanctuary. We worshiped in both Spanish and English and shared together the body and blood of Jesus Christ.

I sat next to a teenager who had no expression on her face. She never sang or said one word. When we shared the peace she would not look into anyone's eyes, or say a word, just offer a limp hand. What had happened in her life to cause her to lose all expression? She did take communion, and she held around her neck a crucifix and she listened to the words of love. Over ninety percent of those from the neighborhood who come to worship went to no church before St. Mary's moved into the neighborhood.

Here is where Pastor Mills, who is fighting his own battle with cancer at the moment, and his wife, Diane, have decided to live and speak words and do deeds of gospel love. Blest are they who sow mercy: mercy shall be theirs. Blest too the peacemakers: they shall be called the children of God. Who are the Mills — saints?

Then we visited Dennis Lauritsen, pastor of Bethel Lutheran Church. He told us how his small church decided to use their basement as a winter shelter for homeless people. People can come in the late evening, receive a warm meal with a mattress and clean sheets and a blanket for the evening. And who are these people? People laid off of work, refugees, alcohol and drug abusers kicked out of their own families for a while, many social rejects, all of them most desperate at the moment. The church started a food pantry for needy families and a used clothing exchange.

Why did they do it? Dennis said, "This is the Word of God, the life of Jesus, and the Bible calls us into caring for the well-being and safety and future of others." Who is this Dennis Lauritsen? A saint? I think so.

But wait a minute. Do you know what he said to us? He said, "This is all sort of easy. The needs here are so obvious; these men are freezing in the street in the winter; they have no safe place to stay, no warm meals. The families that come to us for food or clothes have children who are crying because they are hungry and have no shoes. This is obvious." Then Dennis said, "I know about Wittenberg and our other Lutheran church-related schools, and it seems to me that a lot of kids are going there just to learn the skills to get out of there, earn a big salary, get the big house, and drive all those cars. Students in life for the money. You guys got the big job, bringing God's will and Word for love and justice and compassion to those people. You've got the tough job of ministry. You guys are saints to attempt ministry in the battleground at Wittenberg."

In his lectures on the book of Galatians, Martin Luther spoke about those who should rightly be called saints. Luther wrote:

> The saints do not live without temptations of the flesh, nor without sin. Saints are not stones, or like in the imagination of monks and students, saints are not senseless blocks without all affections. When I was a monk I did often times most heartily wish that I might be so fortunate to see or converse with a saint. I imagined such a saint as one who lived in the wilderness abstaining from meat and drink, and living only by eating roots or herbs and cold water. Now, in the light of the gospel, I plainly see that those whom Christ and his apostles call saints are those who are called by the gospel and baptized. Saints are those who believe that they are sanctified (of worth and purpose), as well as cleansed by the death and blood of Christ.
>
> Therefore Paul, when he wrote to any Christian anywhere, called them all holy and the children of God. Whether they be male or female, bond or free, they all are saints; not because of what they do, but because of what God does through them. So whether ministers of God's Word, the magistrates of the community, parents, students, children, masters, servants — all are true

saints if first and before all things they assure them-
selves that Christ is their wisdom, their savior, and their
purpose for being. They are true saints if they attempt
to do one thing in their daily living: God's will.

Sainthood does not pertain only to the saints which
are in heaven, or on earth as hermits and monks who
do certain great and strange works, lurking in caves
and dens, fasting, wearing hair shirts, hoping this will
single them out for heaven. Let us now learn by the
Holy Scriptures, that all who faithfully believe in Christ
are saints.

With great rejoicing I give thanks to God, for God
has given to me the grace to see not one but many saints.
Yea, an infinite number of true saints ... as Christ him-
self and his apostles do describe, of which I also, by the
grace of God, am one. For I am baptized, and I do be-
lieve that Christ my Lord by his death has redeemed
and delivered me from all my sins and has given to me
eternal righteousness and holiness.

According to Luther and Saint Paul, All Saints' Sunday is our day. The day is for those who have been grasped by Christ. The day where the Word of God is piercing through our lives. Blest are the peacemakers: blest are those who show mercy. Saints not as supra-humans, not persons in some mystical state of moral perfection, but those, like us, in the process of growth, in grace. Saint and sinner rolled into one, daily death and rebirth, baptized children of God attempting to be open to the moving Spirit of God. All Saints' Sunday is our day. A day we share with the big name saints and with those who have labored in obscurity and silence but who nevertheless within their own sphere of influence, repeatedly have been witnesses to their living God.

Today is a day, as is every day, to be challenged by all the saints around us to match their obedience and dedication. A time for us, the present saints, to reexamine our contacts with others, in our social transactions, in the classroom, dorm, Greek house, apartment, in our family life and love life, in our voting on Tuesday, in our allocation of money, and our use of free time, our occupational discussion making, in how we influence others — a day to ask ourselves if we are putting the integrity of our inner selves as saints on the line for our faith in daily living here. As sinners we pray for God's guidance, direction, strength, forgiveness so that our saint-hood may be the dominant force in our lives together — allowing loving interaction to form the very heart and soul and purpose of all our relationships. Amen.

Reward Or Responsibility?

*Then Jesus said to the disciples, "There was a wealthy
person who had a manager of his possessions, and
charges were brought to him that this manager was
squandering his possessions."*　　　— Luke 16:1

Luke, more so than any of the other gospel books, has a great
interest in the topic of wealth and possessions. What part do possessions play in our lives together as disciples of Jesus? What part
should they play? This was apparently a matter of great concern in
Saint Luke's community of faith, as it should be for us today.

The parable of the dishonest manager in today's assigned reading, standing by itself, seems at first glance to be out of character
with the message of Jesus. But remember that this story was ad-
dressed to the disciples — to those who knew Jesus and had experienced his ministry and message. The issue at hand was, "What
should you do with your gifts, your talents, your connections, and
accumulations beginning right now, as disciples? Now that you
know the will of God through Jesus, will you be innovative managers of the insights, creativity, investments, and other possessions
with which you have been endowed, with which you have been
blessed? Or will you misuse this wealth that is on loan to you?"

For many of the Pharisees and others who thought that economic wealth was a divine indication of God's special approval —
a sign of being chosen and set apart for privilege, a reward for their
own use alone, Jesus shot down that idea in story after story in
Luke. For example, in the same chapter as our reading this morning is the story of the rich man and the poor beggar, Lazarus. Remember, it was not the rich man who ended up in heaven at the end
of the story! Being poor is not idealized or glorified, but rather the

point is always that gifts of wealth are on loan to be used for purposes of God's gracious love.

We all, rich or poor, have many possessions. In fact, the stories in Luke imply that those disciples who are really wealthy — really wealthy — are those who have enough to eat, and a safe, warm place to sleep, a life of the mind, and influence on others, which means just about all of us here this morning are really wealthy. Then the biblical witness adds that such people have a great responsibility. Today's parable asks, "How are you, as wealthy disciples of Jesus, going to use your gifts astutely, quickly, and significantly to assist others to be whole, and in that process serve God, the gift-giver of all possessions?"

Today's parable is directed to most of us and the unique possessions we have been given to develop and maintain our differences of destiny like age, gender, race, cultural heritage, different attributes, and quirks, along with our material wealth. How can these be used to bring healthcare and rest and safety not only to ourselves and our own family and friends but also to those around us, even around the world: It is a matter of (as the gospel text concludes) serving God and not something finite such as wealth.

As disciples of Jesus today, how can we assess our own faithfulness as managers of the possessions with which we have been entrusted?

I know of a sociology major at Princeton University who chose to do an in-depth study of kitchen refrigerators as her capstone senior project. The student chose to study not what is *inside* the refrigerator, although that, I think, would have been an interesting study revealing the owners' priorities and extravagances. I would guess one could quickly get a sense of a family's or an individual's bank account, nutritional awareness, environmental sensitivities, ethnic heritage, and maybe cholesterol count, by studying what's inside our refrigerators — there are a lot of possibilities here for a great research project! But this student's project was concerned with what is on the *outside* of refrigerators — what is affixed to the door and to the sides — the refrigerator as a big enamel or aluminum billboard proclaiming the ethos of the individual or family — the refrigerator surface as an open window into a household's mood and values. The study-project claimed that by examining what's on the refrigerator, one can easily spot a separated or troubled marriage or a household that is behind in its bills or a self-centered individual or a family in which the members are not coping well with their self-image and self-esteem or parents who are struggling with parenting or should be.

An array of magnets (themselves portraying various symbols of taste, value, involvement, and priorities) hold in place: lists, memos, pictures, and coupons that transform the refrigerator from a food preserver to a communication center, from the old icebox to a post-modern art gallery of social statement. The refrigerator door is portrayed as a microcosm of the whole household, a message board that can change rapidly as the mood, interests, and priorities of a family change.

I think, perhaps, the most appropriate comparison is the refrigerator as the household religious shrine. It is a shrine that reveals the ethical heartbeat and spiritual faith of a family, as hopes and beliefs are transformed into shopping lists and calendar reminders of intended participation. "You cannot serve God and wealth," is how Jesus ended the parable according to today's gospel text.

Are the refrigerator magnets in your household holding up symbols of service, empathy, and compassion for others — signs and symbols of things that nurture the psyche and the soul and the body of a family or individual and others? Are the grandchildren's or children's artwork praised and hung right up there with Mom's or Granddad's important stuff? How about information leaving precise directions for emergencies and routine caring posted for the babysitter? Do you have the date of the community Crop Walk for World Hunger, the confirmation class schedule, the office blood-bank drive, the church offering envelope, a prayer list, reminders to call a shut-in; little notes and messages of support and encouragement for each other as we search for breakfast orange juice at the beginning of a new day?

All are symbols of our time and talents, our possessions and wealth, that can be transformed into spiritual gifts offering worth, respect, and grounded purpose, expressions of God's love to others.

Today's gospel reading is a challenge to use our gifts with the same astuteness and cunning and energy that the world uses to push its agenda of the selfish consumption or accumulation of gifts and goods all for personal comfort or gain at the expense of others.

The just use of our wealth, possessions, investments, time, talents, and ideas can have a significant, positive impact on the values' development and self-worth and spiritual health of others. That usage can impact our own family members or friends or an emotionally abandoned child here in our community. It could impact a skin-and-bone family whose names we do not know searching for good in the southern Sudan.

We hear the challenge of this parable, of course, in the real presence of a God who loves and knows us and who still offers forgiveness. It is a gracious love, encouraging us to move from being collectors of possessions to becoming stewards of God's good gifts, to becoming managers of our divine blessings, distributors of God's love, and caretakers of God's good earth.

To be very honest, I find today's text to be pretty intimidating and condemning. It does have to be viewed in the light of God's abundant grace. Jesus said to his disciples in parable form that a manager of great wealth — like us all — was summoned by the true owner of all possessions. We are asked by the true owner of all the gifts we have, "What is this that I hear about you? Give me an accounting of your management...." Amen.

Christ The King/Stewardship Sunday
Deuteronomy 8:11-20

Total Living In Christ

In Lutheran churches and many other denominations across the world, today is the celebration of Christ The King — the last Sunday in the church year. For us it is also Stewardship Sunday.

This morning, I would like to make a few comments about stewardship. I would like to look at stewardship from different perspectives, but all the time I'm making these comments, it is always under the most important perspective that Christ is king, that Christ is the one who gives meaning and direction to everything.

In the New Testament, the original Greek word for steward referred to one who was the manager or administrator of a household or estate. The implication was clear. God entrusted his creation into human hands and he holds his "stewards" accountable for the manner in which it is used and cared for — stewardship.

The theologian, Paul Tillich, once said, "Religion is first, an open hand to receive a gift and then second, an open hand distributing gifts."

Most of us have matured in an era of affluence. A generation or two ago, those things considered a luxury are now demanded as necessities.

A person who has adequate medical care, food, clothing, housing, and conveniences — television, washer, car, and education for the children, some leisure and travel — is wealthy. When you have had these things, you've had 95 percent of the kicks from the so-called "good life." No amount of money can buy much more.

But being in this position we seem to be bombarded with advertisements and are programmed to get more, to consume more, to own — but seldom to give. It's often hard today to make the connection between the Creator of all and the products or services we consume. It's hard to see these things as a gift — especially when we think we gave it to ourselves.

There is a section in Deuteronomy 8 that warns us about this:

> *Beware lest you say in your heart, "My power and the might of my hand have gotten me this wealth." You shall remember the Lord your God, for it is he who gives you power to get wealth. He does this because he is still faithful today ... never forget the Lord your God or turn to other gods to worship and serve them.*
>
> — Deuteronomy 8:17

We often miss the gifts of creation. But we are not expected to live in isolation. We are called to live as individuals in community, intimately related to the whole of creation. God's purpose is that all people, created in God's image are to be channels by and through which the benefits of God are poured out to others. The world's things are under our responsibility and management — under our stewardship.

As Christians, we also see and proclaim the gift of Christ as king, as Son, as Emmanuel — God with us. In a complex web of human relationships, each individual matures in a framework of interdependency. We cannot be human alone. As Christians, this corporate character forms the body, the church, with Christ as the head. We become a mechanism then to share the gifts that we receive. The Holy Spirit mediates Jesus Christ to us in our time and place. The result is a faith demonstrated in responsible daily living.

In view of all these gifts of God, can we offer less in return than our very lives? Unless God's overarching claim on our lives and all we have is acknowledged, Christian giving will remain a pious phrase. If the priorities are wrong at the center, our whole life will be out of balance.

Our purpose as the church is to proclaim the gift of Christ, and it is Christ that gives meaning to all our individual activities and goals; Christ gives the "why" behind our personal lives and all life.

This would have to be reframed — management of resources would allow staff or churches to think as individuals. It would allow them to see Christ as truly God with us, and if this God is one of justice, love, union, and peace, then this alone gives us the normative in our ethics. It gives us the base to set our goals and our purpose.

Christ gives us the direction to responsibly use our resources.

It is this same purpose of Christ the king that gives our church the authority to get involved with the education of our children (like Sunday school, vacation Bible school, junior choir, confirmation, youth group retreats) and pension plans for the pastor and programs to feed the hungry.

Stewardship Sunday is a good time to remember all the good things we are doing as a church — because of your gifts. You support the pastor. There was a pastor, once, who was going to leave his congregation after being there about nine years. He accepted a call from another parish. Some of the parishioners were very sorry to see him go. Many others could very easily conceal their sorrow. He ended his very last sermon at the church by saying to the congregation, "The same Jesus who sent me here nine years ago is now sending me to a new parish." At that point in the service the choir stood and sang "What A Friend We Have In Jesus."

The truth of the matter is that we are all called as Christians, to be "little Christs" to our neighbors — we are, in a sense, sent to those around us.

Your stewardship — your management of our resources — allows me to act in our community. Besides my teaching, preaching, organizing, counseling among you, I have also helped to organize an efficient food distribution program for the elderly and other shut-ins in our community. I have also helped organize a recreation program for those with physical handicaps — a program that gives dignity and a future to people.

I interview and direct chaplains at our three area colleges — chaplains that often bring some order and meaning into the young lives of people desperately in need. I am in charge of a program giving scholarships to needy inner-city youth who want to attend

71

church training conferences. I help on a committee that is attempting to deal with the problems of urban decay and dehumanization at a time when most organizations are pulling out of the cities. I meet with and encourage and teach the elderly in the local area. Most of my intense crisis counseling with really confused, hurting people is with your neighbors in the community who don't go to any church but are in need — desperate need.

As any pastor, I do this, and more, because of your management of your resources. Multiply this little bit I do by the thousands of people in churches worldwide, and you can see your benevolent dollars at work all across God's world.

Our church is also called to be a prophet in today's society and to demand justice. We are now telling the community, for example, that a responsible steward of the earth's resources should attempt to recycle those precious resources and at the least, the community should give the citizens an opportunity to do this.

Another example is through contact ministry. Churches are offering the confused, the panicked, and the lonely a point of contact with a person who cares.

Through better stewardship of money and time we could be more involved with all these programs — and more programs that really do give moral fiber to a society that is really reaching out for guidance.

Our active stewardship also is an indication of people who understand why Jesus told his followers to find him in the hungry, the stranger, the naked, the sick, the imprisoned — in situations where guided moral response is called for. Because of your management and your faith, you are working alongside some of our nonreligious allies in the area to serve the aged, the addicted, the alienated, the confused, and the lonely.

We are also attempting to spread the good news of Christ to those around us, including our own children, family, and friends. We are doing a good job, but I think through better management, better stewardship of time and funds, we could do a better job.

I think we have to get over the "keep the doors open" mentality and see just what we are doing — and we are doing much more than keeping the doors open. I hope we can proceed from here to then see the great possibilities that lie right in front of us — now — so close.

It takes a commitment. It takes better stewardship, involving more people. This is one reason why we ask people to pledge today. A pledge card is not a legal document — but what it does is first, encourage a person or family to stop and reexamine their management of God's gifts — their priorities. It allows them to think whether or not what is being given back might just be what is left over. Do we take pride in making things happen?

Secondly, pledging gives the church some indication of what risks and commitments it can take next year. Pledges are not binding — if one's income unexpectedly drops or increases one's gifts will change — but the key is one's commitment to what one feels is important. Remember that money is just an extension of ourselves.

Our identity as children of God gives meaning and purpose to our lives. Working through us, God's creativity can influence the variety of communities in which each of us lives — our families, where we work or study, our neighborhood friends. We must learn to be better stewards of our time and talents — to be evangelists — proclaimers of God's gifts to others.

How do we give? Is it gratefully, faithfully, regularly, proportionally, responsibly, joyfully, and expectantly? We, as the church, are to be the body of Christ. We are drawn together because we think we sense the power of life and because we dare to stick our necks out and say that Jesus is Christ the king.

We don't come together because we all have the same hobbies or backgrounds or because our children go to the same school. We don't come together because we vote for the same people or because we always have a great time together. At times we might not even like one another, but we come together because we love everybody and because the Holy Spirit works through us to make us children of God and instruments of his holy love in our community.

Here we receive forgiveness and strength together in our community and we receive God's Word applied to our individual worlds. This is what your pledged money and time supports and extends. Christ works through our stumbling actions to bring healing to

73

ourselves and to other human beings. Our purpose as the church is to be the body through which the living Lord confronts people today just as surely as he did when the power of life was seen in him in Nazareth — Christ the king.

It is with this understanding of the church that one can talk about stewardship and the use of our money, resources, and time. The only real value of money or resources for any individual is that they enable a person to support the interests of something that the person really cares about. Resources can be used to forward the interest of one's ultimate concern.

True stewardship is not only doing things like teaching Sunday school or tithing, but rather total living in Christ. This means the total giving of oneself to Christ, and this affects everything a person does. It affects all one's contacts and relationships and memberships, every minute of the day. The excuse of inflation is invalid when dealing with stewardship because it involves everything one has and does not have. Giving is gratitude for God's grace. There is only one ground for authority and that is Christ. It's only in this understanding that we can talk about stewardship or the church.

"Christ is the head of his body, the church; he is the source of the body's life...." It is in that hope and future that we pledge our money and support this morning and pledge our lives every day.

At this point in the service, we ask our parish stewardship team members to please come forward for commissioning.

Let us rise for prayer:

> *Father we ask that you help us as a congregation — we who have been grasped by you — help us to responsibly act out our relationship with you in our lives.*
>
> *Help us who sense your purpose to use our lives, our money, and our talents — to generate and to proclaim your direction to others. Help us to see that real stewardship is not a classroom exercise in fractions. It is "What part of our take-home salary should we give to the church?" Rather, it helps us to see stewardship as a homework assignment to total living. To see that total living in Christ is the total giving of oneself to you.*

74

Lord Jesus Christ — who did send out your disciples to prepare the way for your coming, bless now these servants as they go forth in your name in behalf of our church. Grant that the message they bring will be seen as the good news of your action and love in our world. In Christ's name we pray. Amen.

I now commission you as stewardship ministers for this parish — servants and stewards of God's world. May you go forth in the joy of your service and under the guidance of the Spirit of God. Amen.

The True Source Of Thanksgiving

It has been said that you cannot know where you are going until you know where you have come from. You cannot understand who you are until you know whose you are. Thanksgiving is one time that forces us back to our roots — our family roots — and beyond to our true source.

Hopefully, Thanksgiving is a symbol of joy and thankfulness. Thanksgiving is a favorite holiday during the year. Most people like the family gathering and the fact that there is no big build-up to the day; there is not too much responsibility for the day other than being together.

If Thanksgiving dinner is served in a home and not a restaurant, then the responsibilities may be to bring a vegetable casserole, pumpkin pie, and yourselves. For the host, the house has to be cleaned, and the big bird put in the oven early, but other worries are minimized among close friends. If you eat at two, three, or four, it doesn't matter much; there will always be another football game on television, and no one is going anywhere else — unless it is over to another family member's house for more of the same.

For most, the day is a relaxed time — different than Christmas it seems, where there is such a build-up: decorations, buying the right gifts, worries about budgeting money, parties and dinners, perhaps vacation plans, fitting everything in, trying to keep in mind and action the perspective of the simplicity and humbleness of the gift of Christ's birth while everything around you seems the opposite of simple and humble.

Christmas is a joyous time — both spiritually and symbolically — but it can wear a person out. Thanksgiving is simple in comparison and as a symbol, this simplicity is also of key importance. I remember a writer describing Thanksgiving. On Thanksgiving his family got together. His great aunt was there — a very direct, thoughtful, and intelligent woman, a woman who always knew the *Wall Street Journal* better than any cookbook. She was sensitive, and strong, although she had been weakened by angina — fluid and pressure taxing her heart. It had slowed her down; something had been missing the past year or so. But on Thanksgiving, she seemed her happy, strong self again, and everyone was joyful.

His grandmother — in her eighties — was seemingly ageless. She did not seem to get old, especially her humor and smile. Physically, she would soon have to change, but on Thanksgiving, she was strengthening all.

One of his two brothers, who had been searching, seemed at peace with himself again — happy and relaxed; the family inwardly and outwardly rejoiced.

His other brother and his wife and children could not come this year, heading to a dinner on the other side of their family, but they were there in thought. His wife and he had felt closer to them than ever before. His parents were such loving people; he was often overwhelmed by their generosity. They were all together. He could also envision in his mind a similar display of emotions and thankfulness occurring had he and his family spent the day in Ohio with his wife's relatives.

It seemed as though some essential goodness at the heart of human relations becomes more apparent for many on Thanksgiving. Those who are separated from family and friends by miles can sense the joy that is occurring there and know they are a welcome part even though they are physically absent.

Those without family or with families who are perhaps less than they should be — whether cold, or stifling, or culturally removed, or whatever — the many in this position at Thanksgiving can, I believe, more than ever sense the loss, sense the gap, sense the separateness, sense the need for trust and honesty and love at the very center of their web of personal relationships. This insight of a deep need for love at the core of relationships forms the magic of Thanksgiving.

This magic was there, to some degree, I believe, from the very beginning of the holiday in our country. That first Pilgrim Thanksgiving celebration that we envision as the source of our day was a celebration of people coming together to give thanks and eat together. It was a meal of sharing together a lot of good food, not ornate, but good. Perhaps it was more fish and nuts than turkey and cranberries, and no pumpkin pie, but the best they all had, shared together.

The Pilgrims did invite some local natives to share in the celebration but really didn't expect many to show up. The invitation was sincere, I am sure; but somewhat like the times when we are on a trip or at a class reunion and we sincerely tell new or old friends that if they are ever in the area, to stop in for a visit. Very rarely does anyone actually show up later.

The Pilgrims miscalculated. They didn't know that harvest festivals of thanksgiving and celebration had been a tradition among the Northeast Coast Indians for hundreds of years, and word spread fast about the Pilgrims' invitation.

About ninety Indians showed up — twice as many Indians as Pilgrims. The Pilgrim women prepared the food and worried, I am sure, about the surprise guests and the clean up. What made it more difficult was that at that time period in the Pilgrim colony, there were only five surviving women working hard to keep things prepared for the combined party of 140. This thanksgiving celebration was not just a 10 a.m. to 5 p.m. reunion and eating marathon. This first recorded New England Pilgrim harvest celebration lasted for three days! (Perhaps this was the origin of the three-day weekend.) I am sure the five women saved their words of thanks until it was all over, but for the vast majority, it was a time of joy and magic.

They were thankful they were alive, that they had enough food to stay alive a while longer, and they were thankful for their life together. The Pilgrims thanked God and the Indians thanked their harvest gods. They came together for at least three days of interacting and sharing of food and culture. It was a happening, magic, a foreshadowing of the way things should be.

79

Unfortunately, it was not really typical for the times. More typical, I am afraid, were reports of both Indians and Pilgrims stealing food and seeds from each other. Along the colonies shooting at Indians was more common than feeding them. Typical Pilgrim discussions concerning Indians involved not planning ways of cultural exchanges but whether Indians had souls or not. Out of this total history, however, today we tend to honor and remember only the time when the settlers and the Native Americans came together and shared food and fellowship and thanked their gods for what they sensed was good in life.

Today those who are serious about the origins of the day should do the same thing. There is something more here than just the beginning of the Christmas shopping season and Santa Claus. We need this magic today. In the midst of the cruelty of world hunger's effect on the majority of people in the world, in a time when groups of people cry out for liberation and transformation, when international rules are shattered, hostages taken, words of revenge and retaliation are uttered on all sides, when people who seem to have all the necessities argue over insignificant issues, we must go to the center of our lives and our inner web of relationships to find some meaning. We don't know where we are going until we know where we have come from. We don't know who we are until we know *whose* we are.

At Thanksgiving we can often sense the goodness of close, loving relationships. We can sense the magic. As Christians, we are supposed to know the source of this magic, the origin of the hope we share, the authority for loving action and the purpose of the future. It is all grounded in Christ, and yet at times I am weakened and sickened by the rumors, accusations, and the reality of distrust and anger and disharmony within churches and between members — on all levels of the church. I am personally torn between a desire to get closer to the feelings and needs of other people, and a seemingly necessary inner feeling to disengage and look for meaning and purpose on a more manageable level where I am not so easily hurt by people.

The further each of us moves out from the center of the web of relationships, the more vulnerable we become. Yet, if we really do understand the true source of life at the center, we are commanded to move out of the center as vulnerable servants to the very fringes of our relationships.

Today is Christ The King Sunday — the last Sunday of the church year. I believe we should look into our hearts, look beyond death and history, into the hope for reunited life. We should look for the source of our strength. We should seek the message of Christ.

Ezekiel sensed this need before Christ as have millions of others. He saw the demonic in relationships. He saw shepherds, leaders, exploiting the human flock, exercising harsh rule instead of tender care. Just like an early Jonestown over 200 years ago. Instead of feeding the sheep, according to Ezekiel, the supposed protectors ate them. The sheep were devoured and scattered even in the name of God and religion. The sheep were given no direction; no one really cared for them; they were trampled under foot. There seemed to be no source of good, no grounding in love.

Ezekiel then wrote that God promised to establish and act through one shepherd who would faithfully lead and feed the sheep:

> *I myself will be the shepherd of my sheep, and I will make them lie down, says the Lord God. I will seek the lost and I will bring back the strayed, and I will bind up the crippled, and I will strengthen the weak, and even watch over the fat and strong. I will feed them in justice.* — Ezekiel 34:15-16

Centuries later, we sense the answer to this dream — as present in Jesus as the Christ. In the words and actions of this shepherd, the meaning and purpose of life itself is proclaimed.

He spoke and acted with the authority of the living God — a God whose process of creation in love demands justice and care for all the levels of our relationships. It's a source of life at the center that pushes outward.

I know I often rebel against it, perhaps often mixing up the difference between loving and liking, but we must keep primary the insight that the source of our life and meaning is the moving love of God as shown to us by Christ the king — a king who can say that when you feed or welcome or strengthen or heal the least, the lowest of those around you, you do it to me.

Thanksgiving is a time to look at the center of our lives and being, to examine the core, and a time to give thanksgiving for that inner gift of divine love that forms true life. An inner gift that brings the joy that is most often present in our closest levels of relationships, and remembering that our mission, given to us by Christ the king, is to understand and spread that gift of love to the outer layers of our daily life.

We ask God for the strength. In Christ's name we pray. Amen.